COMING INTO VIEW

HOW AI AND OTHER MEGATRENDS WILL SHAPE YOUR INVESTMENTS

JOSEPH H. DAVIS, PhD

WILEY

Published by John Wiley & Sons, Inc., Hoboken, New Jersey.
Published simultaneously in Canada.

For general information on our other products and services or for technical support, please contact our Customer Care Department within the United States at (800) 762-2974, outside the United States at (317) 572-3993 or fax (317) 572-4002.

Wiley also publishes its books in a variety of electronic formats. Some content that appears in print may not be available in electronic formats. For more information about Wiley products, visit our web site at www.wiley.com.

Library of Congress Cataloging-in-Publication Data is Available:

ISBN 9781394359080 (Cloth)
ISBN 9781394359097 (ePUB)
ISBN 9781394359103 (ePDF)

COVER DESIGN: PAUL MCCARTHY
COVER ART: © GETTY IMAGES | HORIA IONESCU / 500PX

SKY10101388_040325

To my wife Elizabeth

CONTENTS

PREFACE: SKAGWAY, JACK BOGLE, AND MEGATRENDS   vii

CHAPTER 1
CHALLENGING MY OWN ASSUMPTIONS   1

CHAPTER 2
AI AND TWO SIMPLE TRUTHS   19

CHAPTER 3
THE FALLACY OF GLOBALIZATION'S RETREAT   49

CHAPTER 4
NOT DESTINY, JUST DEMOGRAPHICS   71

CHAPTER 5
GOVERNMENT DEBT AND DEFICITS: ONE MATTERS MORE   85

CHAPTER 6
MEGATRENDS AROUND THE WORLD   101

CHAPTER 7
THE TUG-OF-WAR: AI vs. FISCAL DEFICITS   115

CONTENTS

CHAPTER 8
   PREPARING FOR THE TUG-OF-WAR: PRINCIPLES vs. DOGMA   137

CHAPTER 9
   A VICTOR'S PORTFOLIO, ACT I: DIVIDE AND CONQUER   151

CHAPTER 10
   A VICTOR'S PORTFOLIO, ACT II: CHOOSE WISELY   173

CHAPTER 11
   CONCLUSION   183

APPENDIX
   FRAMEWORK DETAILS FOR THE INTERESTED READER   187

ACKNOWLEDGMENTS   199

INDEX   203

PREFACE
SKAGWAY, JACK BOGLE, AND MEGATRENDS

COMING INTO VIEW

At 3:30 p.m. on August 16, 1920, a de Havilland DH-4 cleared the Coastal Mountain Range and descended toward Skagway, Alaska—a port town established during the Klondike Gold Rush. The *Daily Alaskan* chronicled the bi-plane's arrival: "There was surely some excitement in Skagway yesterday when the shout went up that the aeroplanes were coming. The first one arrived at three thirty in the afternoon and was seen by almost everyone in town and it was certainly a beautiful sight."

In a black-and-white photograph preserved by the National Park Service,[1] men and women stand frozen in a field beyond Skagway's wood-framed buildings, their heads turned skyward (see Figure P.1). *What did these pioneers think as two tons of wood and steel clattered across the sky in this remote corner of North America?* Many had likely read about the Wright Brothers and "flying machines," but to see one with their own eyes must have been a revelation.

As a child, I would stare at this photograph, mesmerized by the airplane. I could almost feel the rush of wind from the airplane's wings as it passed over my head. But now that I'm older, I no longer stare at the airplane. Today, my eyes gravitate toward the people in the crowd. They were ordinary men and women, living in a gold-rush town clinging to relevance.

That day, in the shadow of the jagged mountain peaks, the future came roaring into view. Were they filled with excitement or fear? I imagine they asked the same questions that we ask when we glimpse the future. How will our lives and fortunes change? Will our children's future be better or worse?

Figure P.1   Skagway residents witness the first airplane passing over their remote port town, 1920.
Source: National Park Service, Klondike Gold Rush National Historical Park, Candy Waugaman's Collection, KLGO Library TA-8-8917.

A CENTURY
OF TRANSFORMATION

History answered these questions for the residents of Skagway. The de Havilland DH-4 epitomized innovations that transformed the U.S. economy. Over the next century, some of these Alaskans might have experienced once unimaginable possibilities—a trip from the farthest reaches of western North America to New York City in hours rather than weeks; washing machines, dishwashers, and ovens and cooktops that eliminated much of the drudgery from household chores. And by 1969, some of those same descendants of Skagway's pioneers watched astronaut Neil Armstrong walk on the moon, a moment perhaps as unimaginable to them as that first airplane was to their grandparents.

Material progress in the United States has multiplied since then. In 1920, the median family income was less than $25,000 in today's dollars. A newborn male could expect to live to age 54, a newborn female to 55.[2] A century later, the median family income is $74,580.[3] Male life expectancy is 74, 80 for a female.[4] And unimaginable possibilities have multiplied, from autonomous vehicles on the road in San Francisco to NASA's plan to send astronauts to Mars in the next decade.

GAZING UPWARD AGAIN

As we gaze toward a future that feels both exhilarating and uncertain, do we see our generation's de Havilland DH-4 coming into view to transform our own work and lives? Artificial intelligence (AI) is a candidate.[5] Will AI disappoint, or will it be the invention that propels our economy and society into a new era? If it is to be the latter, should we be excited about the remarkable feats that AI might soon perform? Or fearful that this rapidly developing technology will automate and eliminate our jobs?

Even if AI delivers extraordinary breakthroughs, there is still the real possibility that technology will not rescue us from the headwinds the economy faces. It will have to contend with slowing population growth, rising geopolitical and trade tensions, and building national debt. These forces—a complex mix of headwinds and tailwinds—will reshape the economy, our jobs, and the financial markets in the years ahead. As investors, how should we best navigate this uncertain future? Should we prepare for the best, or brace for the worst?

Most days I feel like those Skagway pioneers, gazing up at the sky and wondering how the future will affect us all, our livelihoods, and our financial future. But unlike those Alaskan pioneers, we have tools that they didn't—data, models, and the benefit of hindsight from technologies of the past—to guide us in understanding what the future may hold.

MOVING BEYOND OPINIONS

Opinions about our future economic prospects, even informed ones, are not enough to navigate an uncertain future. Just as a patient expects a doctor to discuss the odds of success of a medical treatment when an illness is diagnosed, investors should expect the same range of outcomes when planning for their financial future. An effective strategy must be grounded in a range of outcomes, not conjecture on only one path, and it must account for the interplay of powerful forces like technology, demographics, globalization, and debt that shape economies and markets.

This book introduces a data-driven framework designed to do exactly that. The framework—detailed in the Appendix—provides probabilities of the most likely scenarios that will shape our economic and financial future, primarily focusing through the year 2035. By connecting the forces of technology, demographics, globalization, and fiscal debt—what I call *megatrends*—with the building blocks of economic growth, inflation, and investment returns, this framework is intended to go beyond speculation.[6] Acknowledging the uncertainty of our future, my aim is to offer actionable insights for anyone seeking to build a resilient investment portfolio in the years ahead.

FROM SKAGWAY TO LUNCH WITH JACK BOGLE

My focus on these megatrends is the result of a conversation with Vanguard founder Jack Bogle. In 2004, I met Jack for lunch in the "Galley," the cafeteria in Vanguard's nautical lexicon. I was new to Vanguard, hired to generate insights on the economic outlook for our investment teams and clients. I braced for a debate about the Federal Reserve Board's recent rate hikes or whether next quarter's GDP would exceed expectations.

We discussed none of this. Jack was quick to remind me why I had secured a Vanguard key card and cubicle. "What I need from economists, and what our clients need," he said, "is a framework to determine the long-run earnings and dividend growth for stocks and interest rates for bonds." Jack was talking about the building blocks of returns and the forces (i.e., megatrends) that shape their outcomes. Jack had long advocated for a simple yet elegant formula for predicting long-run (which Jack often defined as 10 years) stock and bond returns:

Expected stock returns = Initial dividend yield + Future earnings growth + Change in P/E ratio[7]

Decades earlier, Jack had noted in his classic 1993 investment book, *Bogle on Mutual Funds*, that using the three components of stock valuation shown here "has led to remarkably helpful predictions of long-range returns" (p. 247). Still, Jack understood that forces like technology and debt shaped these variables in ways that his formula couldn't capture.

As we finished lunch, placing our plates on the conveyor belt to the dishwasher, I told Jack that I would begin working on extending the framework he wanted, a more dynamic approach that would account for the push and pull of megatrends. "Keep me posted," he said. I've been working on it ever since.

PROBABILITIES AND HUMILITY

This book is the culmination of 20 years of economics, investment, and asset allocation research. It integrates insights from three different economic disciplines (business cycles, endogenous growth, and asset pricing) and real-world experience into a unified framework, the **Megatrends Model**. This framework has benefited from discussions with policymakers, Federal Reserve researchers, business leaders, leading universities, and some of our 50 million clients. It is my hope that the end result will help all investors—financial advisors, investment consultants, self-directed investors, and endowments—build portfolios consistent with their objectives.

This book integrates megatrends with the financial markets to present a range of possible future outcomes, rather than a view of simply one future. This approach to forecasting is an asset, not a liability. Indeed, in his best-selling 2012 book *The Signal and the Noise: Why So Many Predictions*

Fail—But Some Don't, Nate Silver rejects such singular "point forecasts" in favor of forecasts that present several scenarios, with odds (or "probabilities") assigned to each. Probabilities are often displayed in sports or in games of poker and chess in trying to handicap outcomes, thus proxying for real-world uncertainty as events unfold.[8] Annie Duke, a champion poker player and best-selling author of *Thinking in Bets* (2018), shares a similar perspective. By estimating the potential performance of stocks and bonds in one scenario versus another, an investor can make better decisions based on the expected values of those different outcomes. By linking megatrends with investment recommendations, this book is intended to bridge books that focus exclusively on economics with those focused exclusively on personal finance.

CHALLENGING ASSUMPTIONS

The main thesis of this book is simple yet profound. It's that the consensus view on the future U.S. economy—a view of "status quo" in growth, inflation, and financial returns that I have sometimes shared—is unlikely to persist. Yes, it is possible, but the future will more likely bring an inflection point. This conclusion is based on accounting for the push and pull of competing megatrends that many standard frameworks can miss. The nature of our work, our standards of living, and our portfolio returns are unlikely to resemble those of the recent past.

This diagnosis is less radical than it sounds. Why? Because the "status quo" view expects a narrow range of outcomes quite uncommon in history. The "status quo" view is close to the type of "point forecast" that Nate Silver warns about. It can be a rational view, but this book is about sharing why it rests on some very strong assumptions.

THE IMPLICATIONS FOR INVESTORS

Whether you manage your own investor portfolio, direct corporate strategy, or manage the wealth of clients, this book has two broad *investment* implications. Both are actionable and practical.

- **First, we should not plan our investments for the status quo:** Megatrends move like tectonic plates that alter the economic geography. The consensus view is a *risky* one in its underappreciation of the likelihood of non-consensus outcomes through 2035.
- **Second, we should plan for two future paths, not one:** Two other scenarios, as I'll share, are more probable than the "status quo." As investors, we will need to evaluate portfolios that are prepared for both. The reality is that these two scenarios are not just possibilities, but *probabilities* that can be incorporated into our investment plans to better control risk and improve long-term outcomes. These scenarios could also prove useful to policymakers.

STAYING THE COURSE

Since founding The Vanguard Group in 1975, Jack Bogle championed long-term investing with a simple yet powerful principle: "Stay the course." This philosophy emphasizes maintaining a well-diversified, low-cost portfolio consistent with one's risk tolerance and financial goals.

As someone who has spent over 20 years at Vanguard, I firmly believe in the power of "staying the course" when navigating economic and financial uncertainty. As the Chair of Vanguard's Strategic Asset Allocation Committee and head of its Investment Strategy Group, I take seriously the responsibility of helping set strategic asset allocations for multi-asset portfolios relied upon by millions of investors. Whether you are saving for your retirement, your children's education, or for the next generation, this book is written with you in mind.

PREPARATION OVER PREDICTION

Jack Bogle recognized that portfolio risks shift as megatrends shift. And while we cannot control or strongly predict market returns, we *can* control market risk by assigning probabilities to different outcomes. That was ultimately the reason behind my lunch with Jack that day. He had respectfully challenged me to use economics to help investors better plan by forming more reasonable expectations of portfolio risks.

In my view, "staying the course" is less about predicting the future and more about preparing for multiple scenarios. Sound risk management means evaluating how one's portfolio may perform given the probabilities of different outcomes. Jack's advice was timeless. This book's aim is to use new data and models to better quantify the risks from shifting megatrends to best follow this advice.

WHY THIS MATTERS

This book evaluates the future performance of several strategic model portfolios under different megatrend scenarios. I'll start with classic ones such as the 60/40 portfolio (60% stocks and 40% bonds). I'll also draw in perspective from other investment legends, including Burt Malkiel's *A Random Walk Down Wall Street* and Benjamin Graham's 1949 classic *The Intelligent Investor*.[9]

This book will allow you to evaluate your portfolio's performance in light of competing megatrends. I will provide explicit portfolio allocations that could mitigate certain risks. I will share why intuitive strategies—like investing heavily in technology stocks during technological change and avoiding bonds during a period of rising deficits—can backfire. If this book delivers on its promise, readers should feel more informed, more confident, and more prepared to take action with respect to their investments and their future.

***

I have never forgotten my lunch with Jack Bogle some 20 years ago, the chance to trade thoughts on economics with this investment pioneer as he ate a peanut butter and jelly sandwich and drank a diet iced tea. Jack passed away in 2019 at the age of 89. But his philosophy and wisdom continue to help millions of investors, including me and my Vanguard colleagues.

My hope is that this book would make Jack proud.

Joseph Davis, Ph.D.

The Vanguard Group

Valley Forge, PA

January 2025

P.S. As author, I have designated that any profits from the sale of this book should be donated to Vanguard Strong Start for Kids, my employer's charitable initiative dedicated to helping children growing up in poverty.

NOTES

1. Gurcke, K. (2012). "The First Aeroplane in Skagway." www.nps.gov. National Park Service. May 8, 2012. https://www.nps.gov/articles/klgo-first-airplane-in-skagway.htm.
2. University of California Berkeley. 2019. "Life Expectancy in the USA, 1900-98." Berkeley.edu. https://u.demog.berkeley.edu/~andrew/1918/figure2.html.
3. Federal Reserve Economic Data. 2018. "Real Median Household Income in the United States." Stlouisfed.org. Federal Reserve Bank of St. Louis. 2018. https://fred.stlouisfed.org/series/MEHOINUSA672N.
4. U.S. Social Security Administration. 2016. "Actuarial Life Table." ssa.gov. 2016. https://www.ssa.gov/oact/STATS/table4c6.html.
5. A definitional note: I use the term *artificial intelligence*, coined by Stanford University professor John McCarthy in 1955, as a catchall to describe emerging technologies that allow computers and computer-controlled devices to perceive the environment, learn from experience, solve new problems, and communicate—capabilities associated with intelligent beings. Generative AI, the engine behind chatbots and algorithms that can produce human-like writing and computer code, is one example. Machine learning techniques such as reinforcement and deep learning, which can almost instantaneously produce optimal solutions to complex multi-variable problems, is another. New AI-related technologies will continue to emerge.
6. These megatrends are what economists refer to as drivers of *supply*. They involve the ebb and flow in the supply of new workers or retirees (*demographics and aging*), the supply of new products and ideas (*technology*), the exchange of goods and ideas across borders (*globalization*), and the supply of government debt (*fiscal deficits*). Other factors I include in the Megatrends Model include measures of climate change and geopolitical risk. And make no mistake—these forces are not just relevant for long-term plans; they matter for the here and now, as I will share in Chapter 1.
7. See, for instance, Bogle, J. C. and Nolan, M. W., Jr. (2015). Occam's Razor Redux: Establishing Reasonable Expectations for Financial Market Returns. *Journal of Portfolio Management*, 42(1), 119–134. Jack referred to the first two components in that formula as stock's fundamental *investment returns*. The latter change in valuations represented the *speculative return* that tended to regress to the mean over time. My co-authors and I expanded upon Jack's framework in a 2018 *Journal of Portfolio Management* paper to include other critical factors, including changes in inflation and real (inflation-adjusted) interest rates.

For details, please see Davis, J., Aliaga-Diaz, R., Ahluwalia, H., and Tolani, R. (2018). Improving U.S. Stock Return Forecasts: A "Fair Value" CAPE Approach. *Journal of Portfolio Management*, 44(3), 43–55. The empirical framework for this book (and summarized in this book's appendix) expands upon these previous frameworks along several important dimensions.

8. The importance of probabilistic thinking and humility in forecasting is also underscored in Tetlock, P. E. and Gardner, D. M. (2015). *Superforecasting: The Art and Science of Prediction*. Crown Publishing Group. Thanks to my Vanguard colleague Andy Reed for pointing out that acknowledging uncertainty is also a fundamental component of wisdom, according to the prevailing theoretical model in developmental psychology. See, for instance, Baltes, P. B. and Smith, J. (2008). "The Fascination of Wisdom: Its Nature, Ontogeny, and Function," *Perspectives on Psychological Science*, 3, 1 which can be found at https://doi .org/10.1111/j.1745-6916.2008.0006.

9. Burt Malkiel's classic investment book, originally published in 1973, is now in its twelfth edition. See Malkiel, B. (2019). *A Random Walk Down Wall Street: The Time-Tested Strategy for Successful Investing*. W.W. Norton & Company.

CHAPTER ONE

CHALLENGING MY OWN ASSUMPTIONS

THE NOBEL PRIZE AND STATUS QUO BIAS

On October 9, 2017, The Royal Swedish Academy of Sciences awarded Richard H. Thaler the Sveriges Riksbank Prize in Economic Sciences, otherwise known as the Nobel Prize in Economics.[1] Professor Thaler, a pioneer in behavioral economics at the University of Chicago, has helped transform our understanding of human decision-making. Decades of his work have challenged the traditional notion among economists that humans and financial markets are inherently rational.

In an interview by the University of Chicago's *Big Brains* podcast,[2] Thaler recalls the early 4 a.m. call from Sweden notifying him of his Nobel Prize. "I look at [my] cell phone and it says, 'Sweden.'" He paused and then chuckled and added, "They tell you the good news. And take great lengths to convince you that this is not a prank." Thaler then goes on to note the call ended with the request: "Drink some coffee because there's a press conference in 45 minutes."

Professor Thaler's work has had a profound influence on me, both as an economist and as an investor. His work on "saving for a pension" and "nudges"—small interventions that help people make better decisions—has added billions of dollars to Americans' retirement savings. Millions of workers now save more for their retirement thanks to auto-enrollment and default features in 401(k) plans, a direct application of Thaler's research.[3]

Another compelling body of his work, some co-authored with fellow Nobel Laureate Daniel Kahneman, helped to further develop and popularize the concept of *status quo bias*. Status quo bias is the tendency for human beings to stick with a current belief or decision, even when new information reveals more likely alternatives. Thaler and his peers have shown that this bias affects decisions as varied as choosing insurance policies and NFL draft picks. In economics, it occurs when forecasters stick with outdated assumptions, reluctant to admit that they might be wrong. My Mom would call that being stubborn. Whatever the label, it blinds us to shifting patterns.

COMFORT IN CONSENSUS, AND THALER'S NUDGE

Status quo bias looms large in forecasting. When asked about U.S. economic prospects over the next decade, I've often echoed the prevailing consensus shared by my industry peers: GDP growth and inflation will hover near 2%. This widespread view assumes a return to the "new normal" world that existed before COVID-19, with low but stable growth, low inflation, and low interest rates.

Having attended conferences for decades, I can tell you that this consensus view is so widely held in professional and academic circles today that it is rarely questioned. It's shared by prominent institutions and government agencies such as the U.S. Federal Reserve Board, the Congressional Budget Office, investment banks, and asset managers. "Why would the United States be any different when that low-growth future seems to have already arrived in Japan and parts of Europe?" the logic goes. Since I have often shared the same view, the consensus has been comforting (I am not an outlier, at risk of being very conspicuously wrong, my inner voice would say!).

Yet Thaler's work nudges me to question this comfort. I am also reminded of what Nate Silver counsels in *The Signal and the Noise* (p. 73, 2012): "Whenever there is human judgment there is the potential for bias. The way to become more objective is to recognize the influence that our assumptions play in our forecasts and to question ourselves about them."

"STATUS QUO" ASSUMPTIONS

I believe the status quo view stems from five entrenched assumptions:

(1) Demographics is destiny.
(2) An aging society invests and spends less.
(3) Globalization has plateaued and may retreat.
(4) High debt levels hinder growth.
(5) Meaningful technological advances are over. The greatest scientific and engineering breakthroughs are behind us.

Of these, the assumption that meaningful technological advances are over is the most disheartening. In *The Rise and Fall of Economic Growth* (2016), economist Robert Gordon explains that technologies introduced since the 1970s have been more "incremental" than those introduced earlier, a trend that he expects to persist. And when Gordon debates skeptics, he asks a disquieting question:

> "You get to keep everything invented through history up until 2003. All the plumbing, electricity, dishwashers, cars, and phase one of the internet—Amazon, Google, and eBay. Or you give up all that for the last decade of invention, including the iPhone, Android gizmos, Facebook, and every mobile app on which your life depends. What do you choose?"[4]

Indoor plumbing, in other words, or a smartphone? Gordon has a point since the answer seems obvious. (Although I imagine a younger audience may choose differently than I would!)

To be fair, some writers challenge this "status quo" view. However, the challenge concerns future inflation, not growth. Several recent books conclude that we are entering a higher-inflation world. In *The Great Demographic Reversal*, Charles Goodhart and Manoj Pradhan argue that slowing population growth will lead to a resurgence in inflation.[5] Nouriel Roubini (2022) points to demographics and a retreat in globalization as the source. Ray Dalio, in his 2018 book *Principles for Navigating Big Debt Crises*, warns of high U.S. debt levels and a sizable decline in the value of the U.S. dollar.[6,7] On the other hand, former U.S. Treasury Secretary Larry Summers (2014) argues that an aging population could lead to stagnation and lower inflation.[8]

A WARNING FROM HISTORY

The "status quo" view assumes perfect balance in the years ahead. Yes, we may see a "little bit" of a growth boost from new technologies, but we could also expect a "little bit" more of a drag from demographics and government debt. These megatrends will net out evenly in the end, producing over the next 10 to 15 years the same growth and inflation that we've seen over the past twenty. A sort of middling Goldilocks scenario, I suppose.

Yet doing my best to channel Professor Thaler, I remind myself of a warning from history worth emphasizing. When big megatrend shifts happen, they rarely "balance out." Megatrends are more like tectonic plates grinding against each other rather than a seesaw balancing itself. When technology and other megatrends collide, one side typically prevails.[9] Regimes change. The consistent pattern is not consistency, for megatrends are rarely in balance for long. An economist's theoretical notion of "equilibrium" or "steady state" rarely exists outside of the classroom.

The 1920s, the 1950s, and the 1990s did not offer a "little bit of growth" or "a little disruption"—they were periods of rapid innovation and disruptive transformation. Growth was neither balanced nor steady; the trend shifted, sometimes abruptly. And the financial markets followed. Contrast that with the 1970s. They were not a period of a "little slowdown" and a "little inflation." Productivity stagnated while inflation soared despite more Baby Boomers and women entering the workforce. In the end, the 1970s were not a continuation of the 1960s. There were no planes over Skagway. The outcomes shifted again because the megatrends shifted.

THE CHALLENGE IN DETECTING FUTURE SHIFTS

Forecasting regime shifts is no easy feat. Traditional economic models focus on short-term demand fluctuations, treating megatrends like fixed constants. This simplification tends to ignore how megatrends—demographics, technology, globalization, and fiscal debt—account for nearly all GDP and stock market fluctuations over the period of three years or more.

A MORE EXPANSIVE FRAMEWORK

This book is about breaking through some of these limitations. Inspired by complexity science, this book introduces a new framework that treats the economy—and megatrends in particular—not as a static model but as what it truly is—a *dynamic system* in which changes in megatrends produce responses in other economic drivers.[10] If we are to paint a realistic picture of our economic and financial future, then small changes in one area of an interconnected ecosystem must have the potential to ripple across the whole.[11] Azeem Azhar, in his book *The Exponential Age*, stresses that such ripple effects and "feedback loops" can make profound, sudden changes in the broader economy.

To build this framework, I tried to overcome three hurdles. First, I compiled millions of high-frequency data points to push U.S. economic statistics back to the 1890s. This helps us capture some of the most consequential developments in economic history—the Great Depression; the rise and fall of U.S. government debt during the 1940s and 1950s; the diffusion of rare general-purpose technologies such as electricity and the internal combustion engine; the ebb and flow of globalization and demographics before World War II. Second, our empirical framework is not stuck in the past, but rather adapts to change. Like a machine-learning algorithm, it naturally adjusts to the ebb and flow of certain relationships and the fact that today's service-based economy and financial markets differ from those of the past.

Finally, and most importantly, the framework better connects the dots by incorporating the three key dimensions of the economy and financial markets—(1) megatrends, (2) cyclical factors, and (3) financial returns—and the causal interactions among them in a multidimensional system. This model is not a magic bullet, but I believe it is a material step forward in forecasting the range of future economic and market events. These megatrends include, but are not limited to, the following:

- **Technology:** I distinguish between two types of technology: *Innovative Technology*, which automates and augments existing human work (like power tools or the assembly line), and *Transformative Technology*, which enables new industries and transforms economic life and society (like electricity and the internal combustion engine that powered the first flight above Skagway).

- **Demographics:** I explore the impact of changes in population growth, including immigration, and the age distribution of the population.

- **Fiscal deficits and debt:** I review shifts in the balance between government spending and revenues and distinguish between fiscal deficits arising from temporary events (e.g., war or recessions) and chronic deficits that compound over time.

- **Globalization:** I assess trends in global trade (e.g., imports, exports, tariffs, and supply chains) and the exchange of knowledge and ideas across borders.

- **Energy transition:** The framework accounts for changes in earth's surface temperatures over time, a proxy for potential changes in climate.

- **Geopolitical risk:** I attempt to account for some of the historical and potential future ups and downs in geopolitical risk, such as the rising trade tensions between the United States and China, to assess what that may mean for our future.

I integrate these forces in an empirical framework that reveals how megatrends affect the "Big Four" economic and financial outcomes: real GDP growth, inflation, interest rates, and stock earnings yield (a measure of stock market valuation).[12] This analysis can enhance not only medium-run forecasts but also real-time estimates for the economy and financial markets.[13]

PERCEPTION VS. REALITY

Taking these insights into effect, this framework paints a different empirical reality of how megatrends have—and will—impact the U.S. economy and markets. As you can see in the table, the framework challenges some common beliefs that I (and, as I suspect, others) have held at some point. I will share more context on these realities throughout this book.

This book's data-driven framework challenges some common beliefs (see Table 1.1).

Table 1.1   Perception vs. Reality

Perception or Belief	Empirical Reality
Demographic trends are a major driver of inflation.	Simply not true. Demographic trends, such as population growth or aging of society, have no strong causal association with inflation.
Weak demographics and high debt levels guarantee dismal economic growth, as in modern-day Japan.	While such conditions can be a headwind to growth, the average historical correlation of either population growth or debt levels with future growth is near zero. Innovation is more important, often surging while demographics slowed or debt rose.
An aging society spends less and lowers rates of innovation as skilled workers retire.	Simply not true. Older consumers do not spend less as they age, although what they spend on changes (i.e., healthcare). An aging workforce can lead to higher rates of capital investment by businesses, a foundation of innovation.
Globalization has been a major driver of disinflation of the past few decades. Its reversal would usher in a higher-inflation world.	Increasing globalization did help lower inflation through lower import prices, although its effects have been fairly modest and uneven. In the United States, this is because imported goods represent less than 10% of consumer spending.

Larger government deficits lead to higher interest rates and bond yields.	Not necessarily, and the historical correlation in the United States is close to zero. This is because financial markets pay attention to why deficits are rising and differentiate between the drivers. (Recession? Temporary or permanent?) When deficits are persistently structural and expected to continue, inflation expectations and interest rates can rise, however.
High government debt levels smother future GDP growth.	Although debt must be repaid, there is no strong causal link between higher debt levels today and lower future economic growth. Our framework better captures how U.S. fiscal deficit spending affects future growth and inflation.
Since the global financial crisis, U.S. trend growth is lower primarily due to slowing demographics.	Not true. The lack of task automation and "power tools" for workers is a root cause, subtracting the most from U.S. economic growth in at least 130 years.
Today's inventions are more marginal than those of the past, and this is unlikely to change. Great ideas are harder to find.	The first part of that statement is true, but past is not prologue. AI possesses the three necessary characteristics of an emerging general-purpose technology according to our framework, raising the possibility of higher-than-expected future growth.
AI will lead to massive unemployment by displacing many jobs.	Highly unlikely. This belief confuses task automation with job automation. Most jobs are comprised of dozens of critical tasks, some of which will be augmented by AI or unaffected by AI (i.e., physical tasks). AI does, however, have the possibility of bringing the greatest change in a generation to the majority of occupations in terms of the shift in tasks of human work.
In an era of technological change, technology-concentrated "growth" stocks outperform the broader stock market.	Not necessarily. In fact, the diffusion of general-purpose technologies has been associated with "value" stocks outperforming for long periods (typically after the initial market euphoria over the technology subsides) as companies in a wider range of industries adopt the technology, boosting their profitability. New technology entrants, through creative destruction, can also erode the returns on equity of technology companies.

TODAY'S TECHNOLOGY PARADOX, EXPLAINED

Technological change is the megatrend that will have the biggest impact on our future. Recent data are discouraging. Since the Great Financial Crisis in 2008–2009, productivity growth has plumbed 50-year lows (see Figure 1.1). Despite the ubiquity of smartphones and social media, these technologies have done little to transform worker productivity, particularly in service sectors like healthcare, education, and finance. The mainstream view is that this struggle will persist. Productivity will remain stuck in low gear. Status quo.

Figure 1.1   A lack of automation and transformative technologies help explain lower average U.S. growth.

SOURCE: Author's calculations

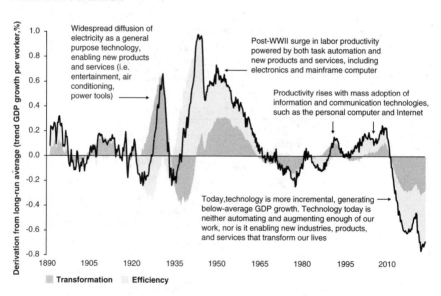

DETECTING TECHNOLOGY SHIFTS: THE BLIPS ON THE RADAR

But what if I told you that we could have some sense, in advance, of whether that was to remain the case? A prime benefit of our framework is that it provides a proverbial radar detector that can tell us whether our future will be an extension of the recent, discouraging past or a moment when a technology like the de Havilland DH-4 airplane creates new possibilities. This radar detector is unable to identify the specific technology or its exact manifestation, but it gives us a sense of the approaching innovation's shape and size, much like a blip on a radar screen.

The unique data and framework in the megatrends model are designed to capture such signals. These signals are not secret and they can be noisy. They are based on how millions of companies invest every day, how technology spreads, and where new ideas come from.

Transformative technologies—what economists call *general-purpose technologies* (GPTs)—change work and life. They raise economic growth for generations. Our framework recognizes that these rare technologies transmit unique signals long before they produce higher GDP growth. Whether it was investment in electricity or the personal computer, the financial statements of businesses hinted at the power of these transformative technologies long before their payoff emerged in the form of higher profits, revenues, and thus GDP. This pattern is a *J-curve*, a term coined by the venture capital industry. The dynamics, famously discussed by economic historian Paul David, as well as Nobel Prize winner Robert Solow, are depicted in Figure 1.2.[14] This pattern explains why our radar can detect signals from the economic and financial future before we see the persistent effects on GDP or inflation.

Figure 1.2   Productivity declines, then surges, as the *J-curve* unfurls.

Source: Author's calculations

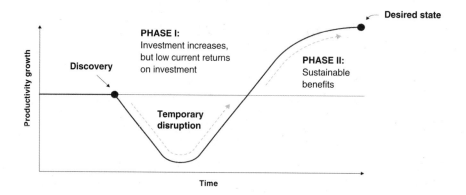

THE J-CURVE OF ELECTRICITY AND THE PC

In 1882, Thomas Edison opened the first commercial power station in New York City. Yet by 1900, fewer than 5% of factories used electric power. It wasn't until the 1910s that most cities installed streetlights and commuter railways, factories built out the assembly line, and homes were wired for appliances. Signals from investment and hiring patterns hinted at a more prosperous future in the 1910s, but not until the Roaring 1920s did electrification drive record productivity growth.

And again, in the 1980s and early 1990s, we could detect signals of a coming boom long before the emergence of the so-called "New Economy." In 1983, *TIME Magazine* named the personal computer the "Man of the Year," inspired in part by IBM's PC Model 5150, introduced in 1981. Microsoft Windows 1.0 debuted in November 1985, though usage remained limited to financial budgeting in spreadsheet software like Lotus

1-2-3. In the early 1990s, IT spending accelerated with Microsoft's commercially successful Windows 3.0. The improved graphical user interface and its integration with more software applications facilitated a doubling in the number of personal computers sold between 1990 and 1992.

Patterns in the labor market and capital investment were changing, but trend growth had yet to budge. *The Economic Report of the President* published in 1992 failed to mention the Internet, even though AOL already offered dial-up Internet services, including email, to users of Windows and Macintosh computers. Yet U.S. Federal Reserve Board Chairman Alan Greenspan saw this transformation coming by observing some of the same signals that we harness in our framework. During the mid-1990s his intuition of a coming pick-up in productivity proved correct. In 1998, he gave a speech on the "New Economy," noting "There doubtless has been, in recent years, an underlying improvement in the functioning of America's markets and in the pace of development of cutting-edge technologies beyond previous expectations."[15]

When Chairman Greenspan delivered these remarks to business school faculty at the University of California, Berkeley, the U.S. economy had transitioned from an expected growth rate of 3% to more than 4%. The stock market soared for an extended period. Inflation remained low, and the nation's debt level fell. The surge consistently surprised the economic consensus, which was more focused on slowing demographics and trade tensions. Chairman Greenspan had already picked up signals of a changing future on his own radar display, just as we do with our framework.

NOT ALL TECHNOLOGIES RESHAPE AN ECONOMY

Many technologies have been adopted quickly over the past 50 years, from microwave ovens and cable TVs to smart phones and social media.

They change daily life. But just because something is widely adopted does not necessarily mean it significantly boosts growth and American living standards. High adoption rates are often conflated with a technology's economic impact. The former doesn't guarantee the latter. Economic impact only relates to adoption if the adoption leads to greater innovation in how we work and unlocks new transformative products and business opportunities. A great illustration of this is Apple's iPod versus its iPhone. The iPod was a commercial hit but not nearly as transformative as the iPhone, which eventually rendered its predecessor obsolete and vaulted Apple into one of the world's most valuable companies.

Over the past several years, AI has grabbed society's attention despite it being well known in technology circles for years. In a short period, AI is now mentioned around the world—as captured by Google's wonderful Books Ngram Viewer—as often as the words *social media* and *electric*. Electricity today is old news, but it was transformative a century ago. But social media is ubiquitous too, and it is tough to argue it has had widespread economic impacts.

From an economics perspective, Google word counts alone cannot tell us if AI will turn out to be *marginal* for broad-based economic growth (like social media has been) or if AI will become a general-purpose technology that *transforms* our work and lives. We need more reliable indicators. Specifically, we need those radar signals that Chairman Greenspan tracked to help us see the ranges of AI's future J-curve.

THE COMING TUG-OF-WAR

This book's framework harnesses those radar signals to project a range of future economic and financial market outcomes through 2040. The rest of this book discusses the basis for—and the implications of—these varied projections. The next four chapters discuss how four megatrends—technology (AI), globalization, demographics, and fiscal debt—should affect our economic and financial future. Chapter 7 presents the diagnosis for the U.S. economy and financial markets.

The coming decades will be defined by a tug-of-war between transformative technologies like AI and burdens related to an aging population and rising fiscal deficits. The outcome is unlikely to be the "status quo" that many expect. Instead, two scenarios emerge:

- **AI transforms, productivity surges**: Productivity accelerates given profound changes in how we do our jobs, driving faster growth and improved standards of living.
- **AI disappoints, deficits drag**: Rising fiscal deficits and demographics overwhelm more tepid AI innovation, leading, unfortunately, to a blend of stagflation and stagnation.

This book quantifies the probabilities of these scenarios and their implications for economic growth, inflation, and stock and bond returns. By understanding these forces, we can better prepare for the future—one that will likely differ from the recent past.

I will also attempt to move beyond the dry statistics that economists can be so enamored with. I will attempt to paint a stylistic picture of what daily life could feel like in these two scenarios for, say, a 30-year-old or a 65-year-old, including real-world questions such as these:

- How may the costs of living change?
- Will it be easier or harder to "get ahead" versus what our parents may have experienced?

THE TRIANGLE OF TRANSFORMATION

While this book's economic assessment may be unconventional, the potential future changes in work and society could prove more profound. I will explore three dimensions in what I call the *Triangle of Transformation*—technology, work, and society's unmet and even unrecognized needs. Every time that technological change has meaningfully advanced, from the printing press to penicillin, society has experienced remarkable and unexpected changes beyond changes in GDP growth.

Consider an example of electricity's powerful impact on almost every domain of daily life, the defining characteristic of transformative technology. As David E. Nye notes in *Electrifying America*, "At home, a young child could not be trusted to regulate gas lighting but could be left alone with electric light, increasing the child's control over the visual environment and encouraging reading. Partly for this reason, the library loaned out eight times more books per inhabitant in 1925 than it had in 1890."[16]

Imagine then how electricity transformed education. A light bulb could provide an additional hour of studying at night for a school-aged child. Over the course of middle school, that equated to *more than another semester of schooling*. All from the simple incandescent light bulb. Electricity did not directly change teaching, but it did enable advances in learning in unappreciated ways.

If AI and other technologies are to prove transformative, like electricity was, they will have to enable meaningful improvements across all three dimensions of our triangle. That means AI will need to boost growth and American living standards beyond simply work automation. AI also must enable *new* services and applications that have their own knock-on effects. We'll consider the potential of several technologies in the marketplace and labs today—ranging from robotics and autonomous vehicles to battery storage and advanced biomedical treatments—through our Triangle of Transformation.

***

Just as portfolio managers and financial advisors need to quantify the risks and rewards of a security or asset class to make informed decisions, we must consider the probabilities of different futures as we find ourselves gazing up at the sky like our forebears in Skagway, Alaska. This book offers a framework to do so, empowering investors to navigate uncertainty with greater clarity and more confidence.

Change is coming. Let's prepare.

NOTES

1. https://www.nobelprize.org/prizes/economic-sciences/2017/press-release/, nobelprize.org.
2. Economist's Journey to Nobel: Big Brains podcast with Richard Thaler, University of Chicago News.
3. Thaler, R. H., and Benartzi, S. (2004). Save More Tomorrow™: Using Behavioral Economics to Increase Employee Saving. *Journal of Political Economy*, *112*(S1), S164–S187. https://doi.org/10.1086/380085.
4. Copeland, M. V. (2013). "Your iPhone or Your Toilet: Which Would You Pick?", Robert Gordon. WIRED. February 27, 2013. https://www.wired.com/2013/02/your-iphone-or-your-toilet/.
5. Goodhart, C. A. E, and Pradhan, M. V. (2020). *The Great Demographic Reversal: Ageing Societies, Waning Inequality, and an Inflation Revival*. Cham, Switzerland: Palgrave Macmillan.
6. Roubini, N. (2022). *Megathreats*. Little, Brown.
7. Dalio, R. (2022). *Principles for Navigating Big Debt Crises*. Simon and Schuster.
8. Summers, L. (2014). "U.S. Economic Prospects: Secular Stagnation, Hysteresis, and the Zero Lower Bound", Business Economics, 49(2), National Association for Business Economics.

9. The consensus view effectively assumes lukewarm advances in AI-based automation (in contrast to some of our discussion in Chapter 2), while *also* assuming minimal inflationary or growth headwinds from rising structural fiscal deficits should technology disappoint (in contrast to our discussion in Chapter 5).

10. In technical terms, my framework treats these supply-related megatrends that determine long-run growth and inflation-adjusted interest rates as endogenous and time-varying. Importantly, these trends are not assumed constant in the future (as is conventionally done) but rather capture critical transitional dynamics expressed in any formal economic growth model. Most conventional macroeconomic analyses may incorporate one "supply" shock; our framework uniquely identifies eight and permits dynamic "feedback loops" from one megatrend to another. For the interested reader, more details can be found in the appendix.

11. See for instance Thurner, S., Klimek, P., and Hanel, R. (2018). *Introduction to the Theory of Complex Systems*. Oxford: Oxford University Press.

12. The appendix provides a high-level overview of the Vanguard Megatrends Model™, the framework that generates the insights and projections discussed here. Additional sources and links are provided for the interested reader.

13. If one needs further convincing, consider the events in the U.S. economy since COVID. Economic growth, inflation, and the stock market have been highly influenced by megatrend shocks, including immigration (megatrend: demographics), consumer excess savings and fiscal stimulus (megatrend: structural fiscal deficits), supply chains and tariffs (megatrend: globalization), and swings in productivity (megatrend: technology). Our framework finds shifts in megatrends, rather than Federal Reserve policy, as the primary factor in the so-called soft landing of the U.S. economy in 2024.

14. David, P. (1990). "The Dynamo and the Computer: An Historical Perspective on the Modern Productivity Paradox," *American Economic Review*, 80(2), 355–361. See also, Brynjolfsson, E., et al. (2021). "The Productivity J-Curve," *American Economic Journal: Macroeconomics*, 13(1), 333–372. In a 1987 *New York Times* book review, Robert Solow noted that one "can see the computer age everywhere but in the productivity statistics." The so-called J-Curve is thus sometimes referred to as Solow's paradox.

15. Greenspan, A. (1998). "Question: Is There a New Economy?" www.federal reserve.gov. The Federal Reserve Board. September 4, 1998. https://www.federal reserve.gov/boarddocs/speeches/1998/19980904.htm.

16. Nye, D. E. (1992). *Electrifying America: Social Meanings of a New Technology, 1880-1940*. Cambridge, MA; London: The MIT Press, page 17.

CHAPTER TWO

AI AND TWO SIMPLE TRUTHS

A TALE OF TWO PROFESSIONS

In 1996, AT&T closed its last telephone operator center in New England. The Peabody, Massachusetts, office was a vestige of a national operation that once employed 40,000 people to provide directory assistance and connect calls through switchboards. "Years ago, you said your name," Rose DiMaggio Trela told *The New York Times*. "You would say, 'AT&T, this is Rose, how may I help you?' It made it so personal."

At its peak in the 1950s, the telecommunications industry employed more than 340,000 switchboard operators; today, that number stands at fewer than 5,000. Roughly a century after Alexander Graham Bell patented the telephone, Rose's personal touch and the job she performed became obsolete. "Mrs. Trela says she understands why people do not need her help anymore," *The Times* (Rimer, 1996) reported. "It's the automation."

As AT&T closed its last telephone operator center, many occupations experienced technological change. At financial firms such as Vanguard, computers and information technology fundamentally altered roles such as the mutual fund accountant. When Jack Bogle, the late founder of Vanguard, joined Wellington Management in 1951, Wall Street brokers phoned the accounting department twice a day to quote the prices of the Wellington Fund's stocks and bonds. Accountants recorded the data in a leather-bound ledger, shown in Figure 2.1, and used 10-key adding machines to calculate the fund's net asset value (NAV, or mutual fund share price).

When my colleague Glenn Booraem joined Vanguard in 1989, mainframe computers had replaced the leather-bound ledgers and slide rules, but much of the work remained routine. "At 4:15, someone would ring a bell," Booraem recalls, "and we'd grab our pricing report from a stack of dot-matrix print-outs." The accountants checked for missing prices and calculation errors. They pulled data from five reports to calculate a fund's net cash holdings, scratching out the math with a mechanical pencil. At 5:30, they keyed the NAVs of 45 Vanguard funds into a Nasdaq terminal for distribution to the Associated Press.

Within a few years, technology eliminated data retrieval and entry. Booraem developed a computer program to calculate a fund's net cash position. The dot-matrix pricing reports and the Nasdaq terminal disappeared,

Figure 2.1   Phone operators and fund accounting in the 1950s.
Source: GettyImages

replaced by data feeds. But accountants did not disappear. They focused on more challenging problems. They became more productive, spending time on "deeper analysis"—developing controls to prevent errors, investigating exceptions, and solving new problems created by the evolution of the capital markets and asset classes.

"Today, there's no manual entry," Booraem says. "That's how you get from 45 accountants for 45 funds to 75 accountants for 500 funds." According to the U.S. Bureau of Labor Statistics, the number of accounting jobs has grown from fewer than 400,000 in 1950 to more than 1.4 million today.

TECHNOLOGY AND HUMAN WORK: TWO SIMPLE TRUTHS

How could computer-based technologies produce such different outcomes for two occupations? The answer lies in two truths that explain the history—and future—of work. These truths emerge from an evolving, often disruptive, story about the technologies that augment or replace our work. Even today, the experiences of accountants and phone operators from 30 years ago give us a sense of how AI will most likely change our jobs, and hence GDP, in the years ahead. This chapter builds on the truths my Vanguard colleagues and I introduced in late 2014 given the broader emergence of AI.[1]

Truth #1: Multiple Tasks per Job

Most jobs consist of numerous tasks. A job description may include tasks such as "organizing events," "scheduling meetings," or "managing projects." A job is at higher risk of disappearing if it primarily consists of tasks that can be automated.

This was the case for phone operators. In the late 1980s, telephone call centers installed computer-telephony integration (CTI) systems. Automatic call distributors (ACDs) helped manage the volume of incoming calls. Interactive voice response (IVR) systems went further, later automating routine call inquiries. IVR systems enabled callers to interact with a call center database through a telephone keypad or voice command. We can all acknowledge from personal experience that these systems are far from perfect, but by the early 1990s, the adoption of IVR systems meant that most calls could be directed or transferred without human intervention.

If you had glanced at the job description of a phone operator in, say, 1980, you would have seen that the primary tasks of a phone operator were tasks accomplished by ACD and IVR systems, namely, to "answer and redirect incoming calls." The list of critical tasks for a phone operator was short. Other valuable tasks, such as selling or marketing products over the phone, were not the responsibility of phone operators. Call centers valued the strong people skills of phone operators like Rose, who politely asked, "AT&T, this is Rose, how may I help you?" but these skills accounted for a fraction of the job's critical tasks. And about 90% of the time spent on those tasks was being automated.

You could have anticipated the elimination of Rose's job if you had looked at the capabilities of IVR systems and compared them to the phone operator's job description. These technologies improved the profitability of call centers, but the gains were primarily through human automation. More GDP, fewer phone operators.

Truth #2: Technology Can Raise the Quality of Our Work, Not Just Save Time

Within the same job, a technology can *automate* some tasks while *augmenting* the performance of others. For example, a computer system can automate data entry while augmenting financial analysis by enabling more complex calculations and simulations. When augmentation occurs, the quality of a product or service goes up, raising GDP as well as the value of our work (did someone say pay raise?). This mixture of augmentation and automation leads to the evolution of job roles rather than their elimination. Our empirical framework captures the impacts of both task augmentation and automation effects across the entire U.S. labor market, allowing each of them to evolve and interact over time.

Truth #2 explains the evolution and growth of fund accounting, as Booraem explained. At the same time that call centers were installing IVR Systems, finance and accounting departments were installing financial software on personal and mainframe computers. Princeton Financial Systems developed portfolio accounting management (PAM) to streamline portfolio valuation of mutual funds and enhance regulatory reporting. Transfer agency software helped process individual trades. Direct data feeds of stock and bond prices by Reuters, Bloomberg, and other data providers eliminated the onerous task of data entry.

Spreadsheet software, such as Microsoft Excel, and auditing and financial analysis software, such as IDEA and ACL, enabled fund accountants to raise the quality of their output, producing deeper audit research and strengthening compliance processes. The accountant's job description evolved, requiring more education or on-the-job training. The increased value of this work was evident in demand for their services. More GDP and more accounting jobs, thanks to augmentation and automation.

AI AND THE FUTURE OF WORK: TWO COMMON VIEWS

Human employment has always involved the acquisition of new skills as technology advances. This trend will continue with the growth of AI, which is advancing in fields such as speech and pattern recognition, computer programing, language processing, statistical and predictive analytics, and process optimization. As we enter what Brynjolfsson and McAfee (2014) call "The Second Machine Age," experts are divided on the extent to which AI will affect our work.

Opinions have coalesced into one of two views. The views sit along a spectrum, with extremes in the debate claiming either of these:

- AI capabilities have peaked and will ultimately have a marginal effect on economic productivity.
- AI will increasingly outperform humans across a range of cognitive/social/emotional aptitudes resulting in widespread job losses.

The second view is frightening. It's that AI will create widespread unemployment. As AI and other technologies advance, automation will accelerate, diminishing the prospects for many workers. In a 2013 paper, Oxford University researchers estimated that by 2030, 47% of U.S. employment could be at risk of automation (Frey and Osbourne, 2013). The researchers later put that figure at 69% for India and 77% for China (Citibank, 2016). These staggering percentages imply hundreds of millions of job losses.

In early 2025, these predictions look ludicrous.[2] Even so, some researchers remain pessimistic, if more measured. Some say AI will lead to job losses in professions once considered safe from automation, such as law, medicine, education, and financial services, including accounting. Some leaders and politicians worry that income assistance will be necessary for the millions of workers who lose their jobs as AI displaces them.[3]

These concerns draw on historical precedent for the near-total automation of work. Perhaps the best example, the diesel farm tractor, is not well known because the tractor eliminated horses, rather than human workers. According to the U.S. Department of Agriculture, there were more than 21 million horses and mules on American farms and virtually no diesel or gasoline-powered tractors in 1910. By 1950, however, gasoline and diesel tractors had displaced the horses, a result of their greater efficiency in plowing fields and harvesting crops.

The other view is that AI will have only marginal effects on worker productivity. Nobel laureate Daron Acemoglu, a leading scholar on automation and employment at the Massachusetts Institute of Technology (MIT), asserts that AI's current capabilities will have only minor effects on the work we do.[4] Today's tasks will be the same as tomorrow's. The AI threat to work will be limited. But this view also implies stagnation in our living standards (low growth, same pay).

This view has precedent, too. Some technologies, such as social media, have been widely adopted yet have given little, if any, boost to worker productivity. It's reasonable to conclude that some consumer-based technologies can lower worker productivity, likely why fantasy football websites are often restricted on corporate networks. Manufacturing firms in the mid-twentieth century were mixed on the merits of having radios on the factory floor, balancing potential safety and productivity concerns with worker morale. Alternatively, there's a clear consensus that indoor air-conditioning materially raises worker productivity, part of the reason why industrial adoption of the technology was so rapid.

The smartphone would fit in Acemoglu's category of a technology with insignificant effects on worker productivity. Compared with in-person shopping or ordering takeout over the phone, the smartphone reduced the time and effort needed to find and purchase products, like a replacement car part or a book. For many of us, leaving the house without our smartphone is more perilous than forgetting our wallet. But the smartphone is limited in commercial application, and for most workers it has saved only a trivial portion of their time dedicated to critical tasks—less than 5% of a typical workweek. These modest time savings mean that the impact on productivity has been just fractions of a percentage point.[5] The smartphone is valuable in countless dimensions, but saving time on the critical tasks that make up our jobs is not one of them. The mainstream outlook for U.S. economic growth subscribes primarily to this first view, that AI will be a marginal technology. It remains the basis for Robert Gordon's pessimism about future growth. He is not alone.

REFRAMING THE AI-WORK DEBATE

Figure 2.2 visually reframes the debate between the two camps. In the prevailing debate, the race between human work and AI is one-dimensional. Human workers and our jobs only move left to right along the automation spectrum. This traditional framing is inaccurate because it doesn't contemplate our moving *up* toward higher-quality, more valuable work. The more accurate figure is two-dimensional, informed by the experiences of both fund accountants and phone operators.

Figure 2.2 Technology both augments and automates our work.

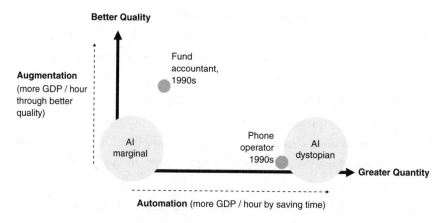

The weakness in the current debate is that it treats the total amount of human work as "fixed," a proverbial lump of coal. When one assumes that all human work is "fixed," then it is just a matter of time before machines will replace all human work. The experience of accountants and many other occupations shows that the current debate is misframed. The number of products that humans desire, and the number of problems that an economy and society face, is not fixed (the latter, some days, seems to be growing!). It's why economists call "fixed work" a lump-of-labor fallacy.

In the United States, we face a demographic headwind—an aging, slower-growing population. More automation—now at a 130-year low— will be needed if we hope to raise growth for an extended period. Yet Wharton Professor Ethan Mollick, in his book *Co-Intelligence: Living and Working with AI*, stresses that AI will not just automate certain routine tasks but should also improve the quality of goods and services by augmenting the work we do. When you read augmentation, think of a complementary "co-pilot," like a Steinway piano for a pianist or a personal computer for an accountant.

The AI debate needs to be explored across these two dimensions in Figure 2.2, not just one.

AI: TASKS, NOT JOBS

Let's see how AI could affect our work over the next 10–20 years. We can replicate what we did for phone operators and accountants for *all* occupations. We can look at the job descriptions of all U.S. occupations (more than 800) and analyze how AI may automate or augment each of those tasks, both today and tomorrow.[6] To get a concrete sense of how AI will likely affect our work, I focus on four occupations: (1) a nurse, (2) a financial advisor, (3) a computer programmer, and (4) an electrician.

These occupations have been chosen for two reasons. First, they belong to the service sector, which accounts for more than 60% of GDP and 80% of the workforce. The service sector includes fields such as healthcare, education, information technology, finance, and professional services. These fields are characterized by specialized expertise and analytical skills. They have also experienced slower than average productivity growth, reflecting a lack of automation. Second, the tasks in each of these occupations are similar to other service-sector occupations, allowing us to generalize some of the insights from this analysis.

Nursing: AI Will Raise Productivity, Support Job Growth

Nurses play a crucial role in providing essential medical care. According to the American Nurses Association, the United States employs more than 4 million registered nurses (RNs), and millions more with less advanced training such as licensed practical nurses (LPNs) and certified nursing assistants (CNAs). As a profession, nursing is not only large but among the most trusted. In its annual poll for honesty and ethics, Gallup notes that nursing has been ranked top as the most trusted profession for two decades.[7]

In the past, nursing tasks have been tough to automate. These top nursing tasks, displayed in Figure 2.3, involve a combination of physical, technical, and emotional skills that are rarely routine or programmable. For instance, an ER nurse performs a diverse range of duties on a shift, from monitoring vital signs and administering medications to making quick, judgment-based decisions in response to a patient's changing condition. Reading a patient's nonverbal cues and providing emotional support are also important in any medical environment. The treatment and care are often non-routine and highly personalized, differing from one patient to the next.

The difficulty in automating a basic set of nursing tasks has meant that nursing employment has risen. When you include LPNs and CNAs, the total nursing workforce has risen by nearly 50% since 1990. This failure to scale is not a failure on the part of nurses; it is a failure of technology providers to develop augmentative technology or the "power tools" that would enable nurses to care for more patients or raise the quality of care with better medicines and diagnostic tools. The absence of these power tools has contributed to weak productivity growth in nursing.

Fortunately, AI has already shown its potential to serve as this power tool for nurses, reducing the time spent on lower value-added tasks and bringing efficiencies to patient diagnostics and treatment.

First, it is reducing administrative burdens and data entry in so-called electronic health records (EHRs), a task few nurses will miss. AI systems are being integrated into EHR platforms to help compose, update, and interpret patient health records. AI-powered systems like those developed by companies such as Suki and Nuance are using voice recognition and natural language processing (NLP) to transcribe and update EHRs. According to two articles published in the *Journal of Nursing Administration*, such AI tools could save up to two hours per shift that would otherwise be spent on manually entering data into EHRs.[8] These hours can then be spent on direct patient care.

Second, AI predictive analytics are enhancing patient triage, including bed and medication management. The Hospital of the University of Pennsylvania is using AI tools to monitor vital signs and alert nurses to early signs of patient deterioration. AI can manage patient flow by predicting discharge times, optimizing bed assignments, and reducing wait times in emergency rooms. In economics terms, this is known as an *allocative efficiency*. Research published in the *American Journal of Critical Care* estimates that such tools could save approximately 30 minutes per patient per shift.

Third, AI has the potential to raise the quality of nursing care by improving practitioners' predictive accuracy and assessing the risk/return trade-offs of various interventions. Medical professionals are human after all, and the benefits from reducing mistakes are much greater than in other disciplines. A recent John Hopkins study estimated that almost 800,000 Americans die or are permanently disabled each year due to diagnostic errors.[9] Another study estimated that almost 100,000 Americans die each year in hospitals because of direct medical errors.[10] Leveraging AI technology has the potential to improve diagnostic accuracy and reduce human error. Research in *Nature Medicine* found that AI systems are capable of distinguishing different types of lung cancer with 97% accuracy and equally impressive results in skin cancer detection. Tools like IBM Watson and Google Health's AI systems can assess patient data to predict risks such as ulcers or physical falls.

The final diagnosis for nursing (and for the U.S. economy) is positive. AI is neither marginal nor dystopian. AI's impact equates to an approximately 20% increase in nursing productivity by 2035, more than double the Bureau of Labor Statistics' estimate of annual hospital productivity growth from 1990 to 2019.[11] For nurses and patients, this productivity lift could not come at a better time. The demands on healthcare practitioners will intensify in future years as Baby Boomers enter their 80s and growth in the number of healthcare workers in the United States struggles to keep up.[12]

Japan can serve as our window into the future. Japan has one of the oldest populations in the world as a result of depressed fertility rates post-WWII. Roughly 10 percent of the Japanese population is older than 80, compared to 4% in the United States, resulting in skyrocketing demand for elderly care services. Japan has long been a leader in robotic technology and has recently begun experimenting with the use of robotics in elder-care facilities, particularly in monitoring/communication with patients and helping with mobility functions. The effect on both patients and care workers has been decidedly positive, such as improved patient care, increased employment, higher worker productivity and satisfaction, and lower levels of staffing turnover.[13] This suggests that robots (in their current iteration) are complementary tools in this high-intensity service sector, a stark contrast to their labor-replacing properties in the routine manufacturing sector.

While higher healthcare worker productivity will improve overall health outcomes by enabling more people to get the medical care that they need, AI might also improve the quality of medical care through superior medical treatments. Electricity's transformative effect in health-care wasn't only through making doctors and nurses more productive, though it did, but also the extension of electricity into new medical tech-nologies, including the use of electricity as a direct medical interven-tion.[14] See Figure 2.3.

Figure 2.3   Primary tasks of nurses and the likely AI-related changes by 2035.
SOURCE: Author's calculations

Nurse

Update health or medical records	**Automated**
Modify patient treatment plans according to patients' feedback and biometric data	**Augmented**
Analyze health conditions of patients	**Augmented**
Train others on health or medical topics	**Augmented**
Prepare patients physically and mentally for medical procedures	**Marginal**
Operate diagnostic or therapeutic medical equipment	**Marginal**

AI Diagnosis for Nursing

Estimated productivity impact: **20% by 2035**

Primary source of AI-related **Mostly automation of**
productivity increase: **certain tasks**

Estimated future job outlook: **Robust**

Future technical skills and training: **Continue to increase**

Different occupations (with different expertise and salary levels) that possess similar generic task profiles and thus similar expected outcomes from AI adoption:

- Mental health counselors (97% task correlation)
- HR managers (93%)
- Recreational therapists (81%)
- Environmental scientists (77%)

Financial Advisors: AI Will Raise Productivity and Increase the Value of Financial Advice

Financial advisors play a critical role in helping individuals and organizations manage their wealth and achieve their financial goals. According to the U.S. Bureau of Labor Statistics, more than 270,000 personal financial advisors provide services ranging from retirement planning and investment advice to complex estate and tax planning.[15] Advisors also add value through behavioral coaching—ensuring their clients avoid common behavioral traps such as selling all of their investments when prices decline. Some wonder whether the future of financial advice is a focus on these emotional elements as AI performs more financial calculations and projections. The history of work suggests that such an outcome is unlikely, an example of the lump-of-labor fallacy.

Recall the history of auto manufacturing. The introduction of the assembly line and unit drive power tools automated certain tasks. Before the assembly line, workers spent a considerable portion of their day physically moving materials. And power tools meant that workers were no longer tightening screws or forging rivets by hand. Productivity in automobile manufacturing surged, making automobiles affordable for the broader population. This automation eliminated some tasks, but it also allowed workers to raise the quality of their output, dedicating more time to work that made cars more valuable. Henry Ford famously quipped that customers could have any color Model T they wanted, so long as it was black.[16] Today, car buyers have more than their choice of color. They can choose a vehicle to reflect a range of personal preferences. And the safety of automobiles has markedly improved with the introduction of the laminated windshield, seatbelts, airbags, rear-view cameras, and autonomous-driving features.

The tasks of auto workers did not disappear when the assembly line was introduced. Instead, these workers engaged in new tasks to increase the quality of the end product. *The time spent by a worker on manufacturing a car went down, while the value of the car went up.* That outcome has been possible due to both automation and augmentation, translating into greater efficiency and scale. In the next few decades, financial advisers will face a similar change in the mix of tasks that make up their jobs. The result will be greater scale in their advisory practice.

Financial planning will become more complex. Some experts believe advisors will use medical diagnostics to incorporate personalized estimates of longevity over time. They will formulate strategies to address the ever-increasing complexity of the tax code. They will place greater emphasis on family relationships.[17] And they will explore the use of data and algorithms to measure our known and unknown risk tolerances. Michael Kitces, a leading authority on financial planning, explains that AI is not about replacing financial advisors but about augmenting their capabilities.[18] AI and automation can manage repetitive and routine tasks, allowing advisors to focus on "real financial planning"—substance rather than administrivia.

AI is already helping. Financial advisors spend significant time on paperwork, compliance, and documentation. But advisors are using AI to automate tasks from data entry to generating financial reports. Tools such as natural language processing (NLP) systems can automatically transcribe client meetings, update records, and even draft financial plans. Automation could save advisors 1–2 hours per day, allowing them to focus more on planning. AI is helping with these tasks, too. Machine learning algorithms can assess spending habits, risk tolerance, and goals to generate personalized recommendations. Kitces notes that AI is particularly beneficial in allowing advisors to serve more clients without sacrificing quality.

Personalized financial advice has long been difficult, if not impossible, to offer at scale. The scalable default has been investments such as target date funds and model portfolios that embed general advice for a particular age group, for example. But AI is making personalization scalable, explains Joel Dickson, who oversees Vanguard's advice methodology. "AI techniques, such as reinforcement learning, can optimize across variables to solve multi-dimensional problems, such as how to manage taxes, spending, and asset allocation, to best meet a single client's objectives. And AI solves these problems in seconds."

That's scaling. Without AI, personalized advice requires time-intensive consultations with a client to review simulations, gather feedback, run more simulations, gather more feedback, and so. With AI, an advisor can tell a client, "Here is the combination of strategies that gives you the best chance to spend what you want while leaving your intended bequest," Dickson says, "Now we can talk about which one works best for you."

Emotional coaching will remain important, but it will not be an advisor's most valuable service. It will be just one tool in a toolbox of increasingly powerful capabilities. Think of a surgeon. Having strong interpersonal skills—a good "bedside manner"—is valuable in interacting with patients and their loved ones. But the patient's primary reason to see a surgeon is for surgery that reflects the latest advances in medicine.

Much like nursing, financial advice has been difficult to automate. Although some firms have introduced "robo-advice," humans provide most advice, work that requires a blend of financial acumen, analytical thinking, and emotional intelligence that can be highly individualized and non-routine. AI will automate some tasks, but this blend of technical and relationship management skills will remain the foundation of a financial advisor's job. Augmented by AI, that foundation will become stronger and more important. See Figure 2.4.

Figure 2.4   Primary tasks of financial advisors and the likely AI-related changes by 2035.
SOURCE: Author's calculations

Financial Advisor

Interview clients to gather financial information	**Automated**
Customize financial products or services to meet customer needs	**Augmented**
Apply mathematical models of economic and financial conditions	**Augmented**
Respond to client questions and resolve complaints	**Augmented**
Educate clients on financial planning topics	**Marginal**

AI Diagnosis for Financial Advisor

Estimated productivity impact:	**20% by 2035**
Primary source of AI-related productivity increase:	**Mostly through augmentation; select automation of administrative and practice-management activities.**
Estimated future job outlook:	**Robust**
Future technical skills and training:	**Continue to increase**

Different occupations (with different expertise and salary levels) that possess similar generic task profiles and thus similar expected outcomes from AI adoption:

- Marketing managers (97% task correlation)
- Substance abuse counselors (95%)
- Supply chain and logistics analysts (92%)
- Instructional coordinators (90%)
- Financial examiners (83%)

Computer Programmers: Automation Comes to IT

While AI disruption doesn't darken the employment outlook for nurses and financial advisors, roughly 20% of occupations will face significant automation and reduction in job prospects. The computer programmer, surprisingly, is among them. The computer programmer has been of the fastest growing occupations of the past 30 years. But new AI systems demonstrate remarkable coding proficiency. Because of the nonphysical nature of the work and the high degree of automation across critical work tasks, some aspiring computer programmers may face a bleaker future. Computer programmers spend almost 45% of their day on programming and performance testing, tasks in which AI systems are likely to surpass human-expert level proficiency in a few years. Fortunately, a considerable subset of these displaced computer programmers will likely transition into new AI-oriented occupations given the relative task-similarity across high-skilled computer jobs.

Early indications of the potential for automation in computer programming are "power tools" such as GitHub's Copilot, a coding assistant that draws on GitHub's vast database of working computer code to help programmers write new code. The tool suggests code syntax, much as email utilities such as Gmail and Outlook suggest phrases to complete a sentence. It also answers programming questions. It can respond to natural language prompts like "I want the screen to display all state abbreviations in upper-case letters" with a snippet of sample code. As the technology evolves, these power tools may evolve into the primary producers of coding output.

This technology is new enough that there is limited research on its effectiveness and the quality of its code. But early indications are that

Figure 2.5   Primary tasks of IT computer programmers and the likely AI-related changes by 2035.
Source: Author's calculations

Computer Programmer

Write computer programming code	**Automated**
Test computer system and software performance	**Automated**
Design integrated computer systems	**Augmented**
Manage information technology projects	**Augmented**
Develop models of information and communication systems	**Augmented**
Evaluate utility of software and hardware technologies	**Marginal**

37

Copilot enhances the productivity of skilled programmers by 26%, on average, largely through automation. A similar product, CodeFuse, offered by Ant Group, is a large language model (LLM) designed to help programmers and has shown to increase written lines of code per programmer by 55%.[19] Multiple studies conclude that these tools provide the biggest boost to less experienced programmers (Cui, Demirer, et al., 2024).[20] The likely result: fewer but more productive programmers, with many computer-related professionals transitioning to related (and growing) fields in data science or other adjacent fields. See Figure 2.5.

AI Diagnosis for IT Computer Programmer

Estimated productivity impact:	**55% by 2035**
Primary source of AI-related productivity increase:	**Mostly through automation**
Estimated future job outlook:	**Decline and/or switch to upstream occupation**
Future technical skills and training:	**Continue to increase**

Different occupations (with different expertise and salary levels) that possess similar generic task profiles and thus similar expected outcomes from AI adoption:

- Computer and information research scientists (98% task correlation)
- Logisticians (95%)
- Actuaries (93%)
- Database architects (90%)
- Web and digital interface designers (76%)

Electricians: AI Will Have Limited Impact

Occupations in physically intensive service sectors are likely to be marginally affected by AI. That's good news for jobs, but it means productivity growth in these sectors will grow at a slow rate. While robotics have displaced millions of manufacturing jobs, these jobs generally consisted of repeatable, routine physical movements that specialized robots could replicate. Current robotic technology cannot replicate the movements of, say, an electrician.

An electrician possesses not only a high degree of specialized subject-matter expertise (an expertise susceptible to AI) but also skills in fabricating, installing, and repairing electrical components in the field, tasks beyond the capabilities of AI. An electrician also needs to communicate with clients and other workers in the skilled trades such as carpenters and plumbers. Unless AI merges in a meaningful way with advanced robotics to fully replicate human cognition and physical movement (a scenario we'll explore in Chapter 7), AI will have a limited impact on the work of an electrician and related occupations for the foreseeable future. See Figure 2.6.

Figure 2.6 Primary tasks of electricians and the likely AI-related changes by 2035.
Source: Author's calculations

Electrician

Prepare operational reports and installation diagrams	**Augmented**
Install electrical components, equipment, or systems	**Marginal**
Fabricate parts or components	**Marginal**
Communicate with other construction personnel	**Marginal**
Inspect electrical systems for defects	**Marginal**

AI Diagnosis for Electrician

Estimated productivity impact: **Minimal by 2035**

Primary source of AI-related productivity increase: **None**

Estimated future job outlook: **Robust and in demand**

Future technical skills and training: **Continue to increase**

Different occupations (with different expertise and salary levels) that possess similar generic task profiles and thus similar expected outcomes from AI adoption:

- Automotive service technicians and mechanics (96% task correlation)
- Solar photovoltaic installers (94%)
- Heating, air conditioning, and refrigeration mechanics and installers (92%)
- Aerospace engineers (80%)

AI will have a varied impact on different occupations (see Figure 2.7).

DISRUPTION, NOT DYSTOPIA

This occupation-by-occupation analysis informs my answer to the debate about AI's implications for our economic future. The impact on individual workers will vary, as illustrated in Figure 2.8. In about 80% of jobs, the level of automation will be less than 50%, meaning jobs are unlikely to disappear.

Figure 2.7 AI will have a varied impact on different occupations.
Source: The author.

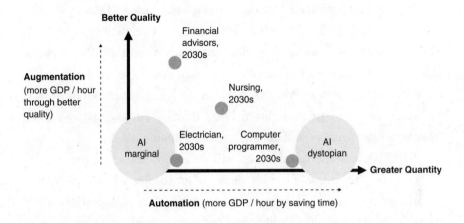

Figure 2.8 Despite variations by occupation, AI will mean change for most of the U.S. workforce.
Source: Author's calculations

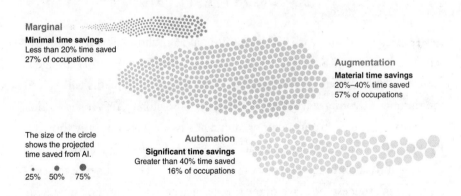

Yet even a 20% change in how we do our jobs is significant. Arguably we have not seen such material change in the time spent on tasks since the advent of the personal computer in the office more than a generation ago.

Should AI continue to advance in its capabilities, a material change in the nature of our work is coming.

But the diagnosis for AI disruption does not imply AI dystopia. This picture makes that clear. More than 60% of occupations will experience AI as an augmentation tool, a "co-pilot" more advanced than the personal computer. AI will enhance our efficiency as we perform our tasks. It will not eliminate those tasks. More than 400 occupations—nurses, family physicians, high school teachers, pharmacists, human resource managers, and insurance sales agents—will benefit from this augmentation.

To be sure, some occupations will suffer job losses in the coming 10–15 years. The occupations most at risk of job loss because of automation are in transportation (autonomous vehicles), finance, and, perhaps unexpectedly, IT. But overall, AI will not be marginal, nor will it be dystopian.

AI AND THE BABY BOOMERS

Between now and the year 2035, an additional 16 million Baby Boomers will retire and exit the U.S. workforce. As we noted in Chapter 1, this change is presumed to be a material headwind to growth since retirements will exceed the number of younger workers entering the labor force. Yet AI shows that we may not have as strong a demographic headwind as commonly thought. By 2035, the average automation rate across all U.S. jobs will approach 20%, equivalent to automating one day of work per week. The bad news: my estimate doesn't suggest the dawn of the three-day weekend. The good news: our economy will be able to generate more output with fewer workers.

Consider this set of bars in Figure 2.9. If AI continues to advance and automate and augment tasks as we discussed here, there may be not much of a demographic headwind. AI's advancement, rather than being feared, would rather come at the right time for U.S. growth.

Figure 2.9   Transformational AI eases the demographic drag.
SOURCE: Author's calculations

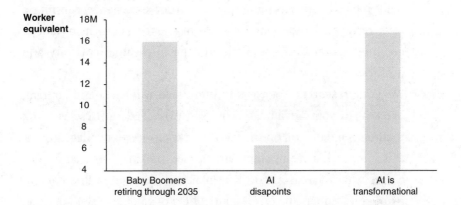

AI AND EDUCATION: SOME HUMBLE ADVICE TO STUDENTS

I have had the privilege of speaking about AI and the future of work at client and industry conferences for nearly a decade. And there's one audience question that comes up after almost every session:

What should my [son/daughter/fill in the blank] choose as a major in college?

It's a good question, especially considering the disruptive potential of AI and the investment (both in time and money) that a college degree entails. It's also difficult for me to answer without knowing the person, just as it's impossible to provide a comprehensive financial plan without detailed personal knowledge about a client. Even so, there are some time-honored principles that I believe are worth considering:

- **Mind your passion:** Note this isn't the same as "follow your passion." We all must balance what we enjoy doing with what we're good at and what someone will pay us to do, to say nothing of the fact that your favorite activities might not be so enjoyable if they were your daily job. Nonetheless, in my professional experience running a large research department, I witness firsthand the intrinsic value of genuine passion in one's work and the intellectual curiosity and limitless self-growth that it facilitates.

- **Do your research:** Today we're inundated with data and content; use that to your advantage. The New York Federal Reserve bank maintains a database on the labor market for recent college graduates,[21] reporting the unemployment rate, starting wages, and mid-career wages across almost 100 majors. Likewise, online content from practitioners in your intended field of study can shed light on what it's really like to work in a specific industry.

- **Technical proficiency is timeless:** The ability to develop or use technology to solve business problems will never be obsolete. Most of us will not need an advanced computer engineering or data science degree to use future AI tools since they will become ubiquitous, like electricity. But we will have to be comfortable using AI technology, understanding its capabilities and limits, and developing the critical-thinking skills needed to successfully integrate AI into existing workflows. Analytically intensive degrees in science, technology, engineering, and mathematics (STEM) may not command the same wage premium as they have over the past 20 years, but they'll still be highly sought after by employers.

- **Intangibles are invaluable:** Social and emotional intelligence, the ability to manage emotions and collaborate with others, is essential in practically every occupation. Studies have repeatedly shown that emotional intelligence (EQ) can be as or more valuable to certain professions than intelligence.[22] Emotional and social skills are not a designated major but are cultivated through extracurricular activities, volunteering, and work experience. Be on the lookout for opportunities outside the classroom that will nurture these skills, even if it may feel like a detour from traditional academics (Steve Jobs long credited a serendipitous calligraphy class as the inspiration behind multiple font options on his early Macintosh computers).

- **The importance of lifelong learning:** Research by the Federal Reserve Bank of St. Louis found that much of variation in lifetime earnings between workers is a result of wage growth between the ages of 25–45. In other words, there isn't as significant of a deviation between starting wages for most workers; it's what happens as the worker becomes more established that determines financial outcomes. View your undergraduate degree as a foundational building block. That's not to say you must accumulate more degrees, but you will need to continually expand your skillset long after graduation to stay on top of changing employer needs.

INNOVATION ≠ TRANSFORMATION

Life is more than work, of course. Technologies such as electricity, the internal combustion engine, and the computer have changed the way we work and, more important, the way we live. Possibilities for a life lived in the twenty-first century are greater than those available to someone in the nineteenth.

Can AI do more than help us save time in our cubicles? Can it create industries, products, and services that enrich our lives, much like the Wright Brothers' December 17, 1903, flight? This achievement did more than introduce "operating a flying aircraft" into the O*Net's list of job tasks. It sparked the development of new industries and reshaped global connectivity. The airplane revolutionized travel and commerce, contributing significantly to globalization.

Chapter 7 will provide an overall macroeconomic outlook based on the future evolution of AI and the other megatrends we'll consider next. The odds suggest that AI will *probably* be the most transformative technology in more than three decades. But for that to happen, AI will need to evolve meaningfully beyond current capabilities to create new applications and industries that reshape how we work and live. The discussion here on AI and the future of work is consistent with that more optimistic path, even if we are in the early stages of AI's ascent.

And we'll revisit why I italicized the word *probably* when I discuss optimal investment portfolios in Chapter 9.

NOTES

1. See the Vanguard white paper: Davis, J. et al. (2016). "Megatrends: The Future of Work." *Vanguard*. Malvern, PA: The Vanguard Group. https://corporate .vanguard.com/content/dam/corp/research/pdf/megatrends_the_future_of_ work_final.pdf.
2. We stressed this point in our 2016 Vanguard white paper, *The Future of Work*, concluding instead that the U.S. economy would likely have low rates of unemployment near 4% and suffer from occasional labor shortages through the 2020s. So far, this has been a prescient forecast, underscoring that our task-based framework can help assess the future impact of AI on employment and productivity.
3. In his 2020 campaign for the Democratic party's presidential nomination, Kevin Yang proposed a "freedom dividend," a Universal Basic Income (UBI) program that would pay all Americans 18 and older $12,000 per year to compensate for technology-induced job loss. Several states have experimented with UBI programs.
4. Acemoglu, D., and Restrepo, P. (2018). "Artificial Intelligence, Automation, and Work," *National Bureau of Economic Research*, January, 197–236. http:// www.nber.org/chapters/c14027.
5. Now think about my previous discussion regarding the marginal macroeconomic impact of social media on productivity through the same lens of time savings.

6. For details, see Vanguard white paper, *The Future of Work*. That analysis relies on the Occupational Information Network (O*Net), a database maintained by the DOL. The database includes information such as required education, wages, work activities, and work environment for the 966 occupations tracked by the DOL. It also uses classification strategies and task assignment similar to other academic approaches, including Acemoglu, Daron, and Pascual Restrepo. "Robots and Jobs: Evidence from US Labor Markets." National Bureau of Economic Research Working Paper Series, 23 Mar. 2017, www.nber.org/papers/w23285; Autor, D. H., et al. "The Skill Content of Recent Technological Change: An Empirical Exploration." The Quarterly Journal of Economics, vol. 118, no. 4, 1 Nov. 2003, pp. 1279–1333, https://doi .org/10.1162/003355303322552801; McKinsey&Company. JOBS LOST, JOBS GAINED: WORKFORCE TRANSITIONS in a TIME of AUTOMATION. Dec. 2017.

7. Brenan, M., and Jeffrey, J. (2024). "Ethics Ratings of Nearly All Professions down in U.S." Gallup, 22 Jan. 2024, news.gallup.com/poll/608903/ethics-ratings-nearly-professions-down.aspx.

8. See, for instance, Smith, J., Brown, L., & Johnson, M. (2020), "The Impact of Artificial Intelligence on Nursing Workflows: A Time-Saving Analysis," *Journal of Nursing Administration*, 504, 200–206; Davis, R., Thompson, K., & Lee, S. (2019). "AI-Driven Efficiency in Nursing: Reducing Documentation Time with Advanced Tools," *Journal of Nursing Administration*, 497–8, 350–356; and, Williams, A., Garcia, P., & Martinez, J. (2021). "Artificial Intelligence in Nursing: Enhancing Productivity and Patient Care," *Journal of Nursing Administration*, 512, 120–126.

9. Davis, C. (2023). "Report Highlights Public Health Impact of Serious Harms from Diagnostic Error in U.S." www.hopkinsmedicine.org. July 17, 2023. https://www.hopkinsmedicine.org/news/newsroom/news-releases/2023/07/report-highlights-public-health-impact-of-serious-harms-from-diagnostic-error-in-us.

10. Kohn, L. T., Corrigan, J. M., and Donaldson, M. S. (2018). "Errors in Health Care: A Leading Cause of Death and Injury." Nih.gov. National Academies Press (US). 2018. https://www.ncbi.nlm.nih.gov/books/NBK225187/.

11. Spitalnic, P., Heffler, S., Dickensheets, B., and Knight, M. (2022). "Hospital Multifactor Productivity: An Updated Presentation of Two Methodologies Using Data through 2019." Department of Health and Human Services.

Center for Medicare & Medicaid Services. June 2, 2022. https://www.cms.gov/files/document/productivity-memo.pdf.

12. Mercer (2024). "Future of the U.S. Healthcare Industry: Labor Market Projections by 2028." Mercer LLC. 2024. https://www.mercer.com/assets/us/en_us/shared-assets/local/attachments/pdf-us-2024-future-of-us-healthcare-industry-labor-market-projections-by-2028.pdf.

13. Lee, Y. S., Iizuka, T., and Eggleston, K. (2024). "Robots and Labor in Nursing Homes," November. https://doi.org/10.3386/w33116.

14. Pacemakers are powered by batteries and use electrical impulses to maintain a normal heartbeat.

15. The number of financial advisors comes from the Bureau of Labor Statistics (BLS) Occupational Employment Statistics (OES), and can be found at https://www.bls.gov/oes/current/oes132052.htm. Data as of May 2023.

16. Black paint wasn't chosen for its aesthetics, but rather it's affordability and durability.

17. There's a reason why a financial advisor and marriage therapist have a high degree of work-task similarity.

18. Lecours, M., Adam Holt, H., and Notman, D. (2024). "Future of Financial Advice: How 2030 Will Differ from Today." Kitces.com. January 8, 2024. https://www.kitces.com/blog/future-of-financial-advice-technology-trends-value-service-engagement-attia/.

19. Gambacorta, L., Qiu, H., Shan, S., and Rees, D. (2024). "Generative AI and Labour Productivity: A Field Experiment on Coding." Bis.org. September 4, 2024. https://www.bis.org/publ/work1208.htm.

20. Cui, Z., Demirer, M., Jaffe, S., Musolff, L., Peng, S., and Salz, T. (2024). "The Effects of Generative AI on High Skilled Work: Evidence from Three Field Experiments with Software Developers," January. https://doi.org/10.2139/ssrn.4945566.

21. https://www.newyorkfed.org/research/college-labor-market#--:explore:unemployment.

22. Deming, D. J. (2016). *The Growing Importance of Social Skills in the Labor Market.* Working Paper No. 21473. Cambridge, Massachusetts: National Bureau of Economic Research.

CHAPTER THREE

THE FALLACY OF GLOBALIZATION'S RETREAT

THE MIRACLE OF MODERN COMMERCE

On the outskirts of Zhengzhou, China, a massive industrial complex stretches across more than 2 square miles. Locals call it "iPhone City." Operated by Foxconn, the manufacturing facility produces more than 500,000 iPhones a day, or more than half of all iPhones sold globally. The site is the final link in a global supply chain captured by a slogan etched into early iPhones: "Designed by Apple in California. Assembled in China."[1]

The iPhone and the supply chain that produces it are a miracle of modern commerce—a complex coordination of design, engineering, and manufacturing to make a supercomputer that fits in our pockets. In 2000, the fastest supercomputer—the IBM ASCI White—performed 4.9 trillion operations per second, but it weighed 106 tons and cost $183 million in today's dollars.[2] The iPhone 15 performs 35 trillion operations per second, fits in your pocket, and costs less than $1,000.[3]

How did we get from a 106-ton supercomputer to an 8-ounce smartphone? Part of the answer is innovation. But part of that innovation is globalization. Foxconn's Zhengzhou facility can serve as a symbol of a roughly 50-year surge in global trade and global supply chains, a development illustrated by the *New York Times* columnist Thomas L. Friedman in his 2005 book *The World Is Flat*. He recounts a visit with Dick Hunter, the global production manager at Dell, provider of Friedman's Inspiron 600m notebook. He asks Hunter where his notebook comes from.

The answer: the design from Austin, Texas, and Taipei, Taiwan; the wireless card from Malaysia; the microprocessor from Costa Rica, Malaysia, or China; the microchips from the Philippines, Costa Rica, Malaysia, or China; the memory cards from Korea, Germany, or Japan; the modem from a Foxconn plant in China; and on and on until a Dell plant in Penang, Malaysia, assembles the components into Friedman's laptop.[4]

THE FEAR OF GLOBALIZATION'S RETREAT

But global supply chains and their commercial miracles are now under pressure. Geopolitical tensions between the United States and China, trade restrictions, and hikes in tariffs are sparking growing concern that globalization's retreat is inevitable. Some economists, including Nouriel Roubini in his 2022 book *Megathreats*, warn that rising protectionism and "slowbalization" could trigger a prolonged stagflationary era—an unpleasant combination of slower growth and higher inflation. Goodhart and Pradhan (2020) argue that a retreat from globalization, when combined with aging populations, will lead to an era of higher inflation.[5]

If globalization has driven down inflation for decades, won't its retreat drive prices up? If global supply chains boost efficiency, won't reshoring drive costs higher? These arguments seem logical. But they're overstated.

THE TRADITIONAL GLOBALIZATION STORY FALLS APART

There are two critical flaws in the argument that "slowbalization" will lead to stagflation. First, the impact of globalization on U.S. inflation is modest. Globalization clearly enriches our lives, and imports play a role in prices. I would struggle to start my day in Pennsylvania without coffee imported from Brazil. But imports account for less than 10% of U.S. consumer spending, limiting their impact on the broad economy. (Trade plays a larger role in other developed economies.) In other words, the step back from globalization would have to be incredibly large to produce such worrisome outcomes. Second, and most important, the focus on trade in goods and services and foreign direct investment ignores globalization's most important dimension: the exchange of ideas. And unlike trade in goods, the trade in ideas is accelerating.

WHAT THE DATA SAY

Economic headlines can make globalization seem like an unstoppable force, its orbit forever expanding. Since 1870, however, levels of trade and foreign investment have risen and fallen. Until 2007, global trade and cross-border capital flows, as a percentage of GDP, were highest in the late nineteenth and early twentieth centuries. Global trade surged, powered by breakthroughs in transportation and communication such as oceangoing steamships, railroads, and telegraph lines that connected continents.

Globalization then collapsed. Protectionist policies such as the U.S. Smoot-Hawley Tariff Act of 1930, retaliatory tariffs, and two World Wars drove global trade to modern lows.[6] Even in 1975, exports and imports as a fraction of economic output remained below levels recorded by Britain during the late nineteenth and early twentieth centuries. The 1980s marked the start of a new globalization era, culminating in China's 2001 ascension to the World Trade Organization (WTO). On the eve of the 2008–2009 Global Financial Crisis, global trade as a percentage of economic output surpassed its early- twentieth-century highs. Since then, it has stalled, fanning fears that "slowbalization" will mean permanently lower growth and persistently higher inflation.

The data tells a different story. This book's megatrends framework reveals that changes in the levels of globalization have had a modest impact on U.S. economic and financial outcomes. Even inflation, which would seem susceptible to changes in the volume of trade, has been more sensitive to other drivers. Consider Figure 3.1, which compares actual U.S. inflation with what it would have been without any increase in globalization over the past 30+ years.

The picture from our root-cause analysis is clear: globalization has lowered U.S. inflation, but only by a modest amount. Since 1980, the era of globalization's impact, which includes global supply chains stretching from Cupertino, California to Zhengzhou, China, has been mixed. Before 2001, when China joined the World Trade Organization (WTO), changes in globalization nudged inflation marginally higher, adding an average of 9 basis points (bps) per year to changes in the consumer price index. (One basis point is 1/100th of a percentage point.) Since 2002 and what economists call "the China shock," the impact has been more pronounced and deflationary. Globalization has shaved, on average, 27 bps from the annual inflation rate. That means that rather than inflation having been, say, 2% per year, it would have been 2.27%. Higher, but not dramatically so.

Figure 3.1 Increased globalization of trade has modestly lowered inflation.

Notes: The figure shows year-on-year inflation (black) between 1987 and the third quarter of 2023, and hypothetical inflation, assuming that the globalization driver equaled zero over that period. The light grey shaded area represents the difference between the two lines, such that a positive (negative) value indicates that realized inflation was higher (lower) due to the impact of the changes in globalization.

Source: Author's calculations, as of May 2024

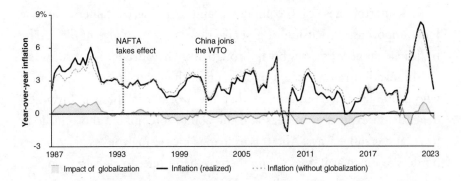

These insights are consistent with the past 130 years of U.S. trade. Globalization changes have accounted for only 13% of changes in the inflation rate, or 13 cents for every $1 change in our costs of living. That impact is not inconsequential, but neither is it cause for concern that "slowbalization" will fuel a persistent, multi-year surge in inflation. The most important driver of price changes has been monetary and fiscal policy, accounting for more than 70% of changes in the price level.

Trade's contribution to growth has been similarly modest, in part due to offsetting effects. While lower import prices has supported consumption and corporate profits, our framework finds that globalization has also reduced domestic investment, all else equal. Overall, rising globalization has accounted for 10% of the changes in U.S. real growth since 1890.[7] The most important driver has been changes in technology, by a ratio of more than 4:1. But let's not rush to conclude that only domestic innovation matters. That would be a mistake. For innovation is a global process.

53

GLOBALIZATION'S REAL GROWTH ENGINE: THE TRADE IN IDEAS

For too long, discussions of globalization have been centered on physical trade—smartphones, cars, computers, and shipping containers. But the most important dimension of globalization is the *exchange of ideas*. The trade in ideas powers every breakthrough, from new drugs to new software.

Innovation rarely occurs in a vacuum, the product of a lone genius who stumbles upon an insight that the world has missed. Invention depends on exposure to ideas and the ability to combine those ideas in novel and creative ways. And this exchange increasingly takes place *across* borders as much as it does *within* them. When I refer to *globalization*, this is the dimension that I have in mind.[8]

Marc Levinson, in his 2020 book *Outside the Box: How Globalization Changed from Moving Stuff to Spreading Ideas*, compares globalization in goods to the (more amorphous) trade in ideas and knowledge. Levinson compares the growth in the number of shipping containers that a cargo ship can hold versus the rate of sharing scientific knowledge around the world. Consider the following average growth rate along these two dimensions of globalization:

- **Goods:** Growth in shipping containers per cargo ship: 7% per year
- **Ideas:** Growth in scientific research downloaded: 19% per year

In 1956, the first cargo ship held 226 containers; today, the largest cargo ships hold more than 24,000 containers, an increase in trade capacity of more than 7% per year. But that growth pales in comparison to the rate of sharing of scientific knowledge.[9] In November 2024, more than 54 million papers across a range of disciplines were downloaded from academic sharing network arXiv.org, up from an average of just 500,000 in 1999. Unlike a shipping container, which can be in only one place at one time, an idea can be in a million places at once.

Experts have long recognized that knowledge exchange is a contributor to productivity growth.[10] This dimension of globalization holds more potential to raise U.S. GDP than trade in physical goods and commodities. By changing our perspective on globalization, I aim to convince you that globalization, like AI, could be a tailwind to future global growth, a dimension uncovered in most stories about globalization.

To prove this, I set out to trace every meaningful and influential idea circulating around the world over the past 20 years or so. This was no small feat, considering that there are more than 2 billion records of innovation that I attempted to capture. This effort helps chart globalization's future direction and the specific fields in which the next great idea, perhaps enabled by AI, may come from.

But first I need to illustrate what I mean by the trade in ideas. I start with the Wright brothers' airplane, a precursor to the de Havilland DH-4 that flew over Skagway, Alaska. I then return to the present with the Apple iPhone.

TRADE IN IDEAS CRITICAL TO MAN'S FIRST FLIGHT

The more knowledge people are exposed to, the greater the odds they will create a new idea themselves. That's why education is so important. The British band The Fixx had a hit single in 1983 called "One Thing Leads to Another." I don't know whether that band was referring to ideas. If so, they were right. One idea leads to another. And when ideas in a certain field reach critical mass, they make the transformative potential of commercial technologies more likely.

For years, my family and I have spent summer vacations in the Outer Banks of North Carolina. Every time I pass the Wright Brothers Museum on Route 158 in Kitty Hawk, North Carolina, I think about December 17, 1903. On that day, Orville Wright soared above the earth's surface in a heavier-than-air aircraft at a top speed of 6.8 miles per hour. Fifty-nine seconds of flight that changed the world.

How did the Wright brothers—bicycle mechanics from Dayton, Ohio—manage this feat? David McCullough, in his masterful 2015 book *The Wright Brothers*, identifies no single light-bulb "eureka" moment, but he highlights a turning point prompted by an idea from France. In 1899, the Commissioner of the U.S. Patent Office (infamously) said, "Everything that can be invented has been invented." That same year, Wilbur Wright wrote a two-page letter to the United States' Smithsonian Institution stating: "I wish to avail myself of all that is known about aviation."

This letter kick-started a chain reaction. The Wright Brothers received dozens of articles and books from the Smithsonian and the scientific community. Yet for the Wright Brothers, the most important idea in that network was imported. It came from a French book entitled *Empire of the Air* that the Smithsonian had sent them. It was an aviation book—on *birds*. Yes, the Smithsonian had sent the Wright brothers a bird book. Before you laugh, we should recall that humans at that time couldn't yet fly.

Exposure to that ornithological research, depicted in Figure 3.2, inspired the Wright Brothers to mimic the twist in birds' wings and create a more aerodynamic wing for their airplane. That change in wing design led them to their patented rudder system.

One idea from France led to a more significant one on a beach in North Carolina. The Wright Brothers were nearly alone on that remote beach the day of man's first flight, but they didn't go it alone. The exchange of knowledge across cities and countries made human's first flight possible.

Figure 3.2   Ornithological research helped the Wright brothers develop their airplane wing

SOURCE: Animal locomotion; or walking, swimming, and flying with a dissertation on aeronautics by James Bell Pettigrew (1874), and the Library of Congress

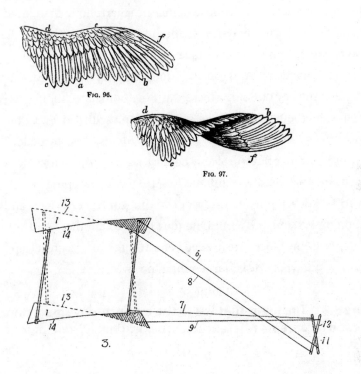

SUPPLY CHAIN OF IDEAS PROPELLED THE IPHONE

Fast-forward to today, and you will see the same pattern with the iPhone. As it rolls off a Zhengzhou assembly line, Apple's iPhone is less a collection of components than an integration of ideas. Apple patented the first-generation iPhone in 2006. Figure 3.3 depicts the network of ideas cited in its patent application. You'll notice more than 100 previous ideas that were instrumental in the development of the first iPhone. The ideas were from numerous fields, ranging from automatic data compression to zooming functionality. Two things have changed over the past century.

The first is that the exchange of knowledge is more global. This global trade has mattered more for developing the smartphone than it did for the airplane. Second, this analysis reframes ideas as building blocks. Each line in this network represents a key idea—a building block—critical to making the smartphone work. And each building block has its own idea network.

One of the key building blocks was Bluetooth, a technology created in Sweden. Bluetooth can trace its origins, along with Wi-Fi, to the 1940s, from ideas for torpedo radio guidance systems. Yes, torpedoes led to Bluetooth. (Strange but true: Hedy Lamarr, a glamorous star in Hollywood's Golden Age, patented a technique for "frequency hopping" that contributed to the development of torpedo radio guidance, Wi-Fi, and global positioning systems (GPS).)[11] One idea leads to another. And sometimes multiple building blocks are needed before there can be a great leap forward in innovation, when ideas start coming in waves.

Figure 3.3 The ideas that led to the modern-day smart phone (location of patents referenced in the original iPhone patent registration)

Notes: Thickness of lines represents the quantity of patents
Source: Vanguard calculations, based on data from Google Patents

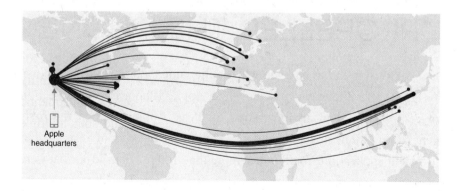

And increasingly, those building blocks are not concentrated in any one country. This is the untold story of globalization. The emergence of idea building blocks helps to explain why innovation cycles up and down, in long waves. The key is knowing where the global wave of ideas is headed. Could AI find an ally in the pursuit of higher U.S. economic growth? Let's find out.

THE IDEA MULTIPLIER: A GLOBAL TRACKING SYSTEM

Measuring ideas and their evolution may seem like an abstract concept. Ideas are not statistics. But we can trace ideas through research and development, patents, and scientific papers. A relatively recent innovation that facilitates the sharing of ideas (the Internet) allows us to quantify the development and transmission of ideas throughout industries and countries by tracking patents and academic journal citations. Journals, such as the *New England Journal of Medicine*, act as a base camp where ideas are articulated and debated before firms invest heavily in R&D and any patents are granted.

Some ideas come from the private sector, others from universities or government agencies. But all are built on a foundation of existing ideas. A select few go on to be great themselves or to serve as building blocks for the future. And I don't wish to capture just any idea. The goal is to identify and trace groundbreaking ideas, since these represent a fundamental building block of innovation. And it is these that should spur multiple future ideas. Watson and Crick's famous 1953 paper in *Nature* on DNA's double-helix structure, for instance, is among the most cited articles of all time. When ideas are that influential, other ideas are more likely to follow.

In previous research, I used the Clarivate Analytics Web of Science platform, a global citation database with more than 1.7 billion data points designed to track citations for faculty and other researchers around the world. From this database we can calculate what I call the **Idea Multiplier** to measure how many future ideas are sparked by one idea today.

The idea multiplier is designed to detect critical mass. In previous research, my Vanguard colleagues and I demonstrated a statistically significant relationship between changes in the idea multiplier and subsequent changes in productivity for both industries and countries. A doubling of the idea multiplier can lead to a 1.2 percentage point change in productivity growth over the next five years. In other words, the exchange of ideas is a leading indicator of technological change, with impacts similar to those discussed in our J-curve assessment of the impact of new technologies.

THE EXCHANGE OF IDEAS IS ACCELERATING

We can see how much the world of ideas is changing by tracing the idea multiplier over time. I focus on the five largest countries. In 2000, the United States, representing just 5% of the world's population, generated 50% of the world's ideas. China, 21% of the world's population, contributed only 4% of the world's ideas. Japan, the United Kingdom, and Germany, with a combined 4% of the world's population, produced 23% of the world's ideas.

There were fewer ideas in 2000, and it was not because of technology. We had the Internet back then, so we had access to information. The Internet does not create new ideas; it just makes them easier to download. There were fewer ideas in 2000 because the United States accounted for a disproportionate share of creativity, and the exchange of knowledge went in only one direction.

Today, distances are shrinking fast, and two-way knowledge exchange is accelerating. China now plays a crucial role in the global idea multiplier, with its innovations inspiring ideas across multiple sectors worldwide. For example, in 2021, China became the largest contributor to global research publications, accounting for 23.4% of the world's research papers, surpassing the United States. Additionally, China leads the world in international patent filings, contributing nearly 50% of global patent applications in 2022. Many of China's technological advances in fields like AI, fintech, and biotechnology serve as the foundation for further innovations in countries such as the United States, Germany, and Japan.

There are three primary reasons for this pickup:

- The rise of China's knowledge economy
- More idea building blocks
- The cross-pollination of ideas

THE RISE OF CHINA'S KNOWLEDGE ECONOMY

Chinese researchers and entrepreneurs have expanded the frontiers of financial technology (fintech) and healthcare research. In 2020, 87% of China's population used mobile payment apps, compared with less than 40% in the United States. Alipay and WeChat Pay, China's largest mobile payment platforms, process more than $40 trillion in transactions annually, digital payments for everything from your morning coffee to your share of the tab for dinner with friends. In 2023, PayPal, a similar U.S. service, processed just $1.5 trillion in transactions.[12]

Biotechnology is also booming. Chinese companies now conduct more clinical trials for new drugs than any other country. Investment in genomics and personalized medicine has resulted in therapies like Bei Gene's cancer drug, recently approved by the U.S. FDA. Faster drug development, particularly in the face of China's rapidly aging population, has significant economic implications. By 2040, more than 28% of China's population will be 60 or older, intensifying pressure on healthcare systems and government spending. The ability to quickly develop new therapies through AI-driven drug discovery and advanced biologics could reduce the financial burden on the healthcare system by treating age-related diseases more effectively. For example, early treatment of chronic diseases like Alzheimer's and diabetes could potentially save China's healthcare system billions—by some estimates, up to 3% of GDP annually—by lowering long-term care costs and reducing hospitalizations. These innovations are essential in mitigating the growing fiscal challenges posed by an aging society.

MORE IDEA BUILDING BLOCKS

The digital and AI revolution has created tools for innovation and idea generation. Machine learning algorithms, coupled with cloud computing, have lowered barriers to entry for research and innovation. In the past, researchers relied on expensive proprietary software or hardware. But platforms like Google's TensorFlow and Microsoft's Azure AI offer lower-cost open-source AI tools accessible to anyone with an Internet connection.

GitHub, the world's largest open-source code repository for software developers, has 100 million developers scattered across the globe. As noted in Chapter 2, tools such as GitHub's Copilot help developers capitalize on this global expertise to write new code. Early indications are that Copilot enhances the productivity of skilled programmers by 26%, on average, largely through automation. Copilot and similar tools provide the biggest boost to less experienced programmers.

Data is another "building block." By 2025, the global economy will generate 181 zettabytes of data, up from 64 zettabytes in 2020. What is a zettabyte? A high-definition recording of every word ever spoken by humanity. These data are fuel that AI engines can use to synthesize new insights.

CROSS-POLLINATION OF IDEAS

In bioinformatics, the integration of biological and data science is leading to groundbreaking discoveries. The Human Genome Project, completed in 2003, is the most famous large-scale interdisciplinary project, requiring collaboration among geneticists, computer scientists, and statisticians. The results of this effort continue to pay dividends: AI-driven genomics allows for the possibility of personalized medicine, a market expected to grow by 20% annually in the next decade.

In the financial services industry, fintech companies blend expertise from economics, computer science, and behavioral psychology to create systems to predict markets and execute trades more efficiently. By 2023, algorithmic trading accounted for nearly 70% of all trading volume in the U.S. stock markets.

Interdisciplinary collaboration is also driving sustainability initiatives. Environmental scientists now work with data scientists to use AI and machine learning to model climate change. IBM's Green Horizon Project, for example, uses AI to predict air pollution levels and optimize renewable energy resources. Startups like Indigo Agriculture apply AI and microbiome research to increase crop resilience, reduce the use of fertilizers, and cut greenhouse gas emissions.

Today, more than 50% of the world's ideas would not have been possible without the global exchange of knowledge. The increase in international knowledge sharing is responsible for more than half of all new scientific discoveries since that time. That's the power of globalization.

The result? The number of ideas is accelerating in every country. A medical idea in Japan now leads to more medical ideas in the United States, China, and Germany. When an idea is created in Vegas, it doesn't stay in Vegas. And that's a good thing because the trade of ideas is not a zero-sum game. When I use a barrel of oil, I exhaust it. When I use an idea, I don't. You can use it too.

The *Idea Multiplier*, a leading indicator of innovation, predicts innovation up to five years into the future. The ideas in our multiplier haven't yet been commercialized into GDP; the ideas are in the R&D lab, in clinical trials, and in universities and patent applications. Ideas in the multiplier are still incubating.

The idea multiplier's definition is simple: it indicates how many subsequent good ideas are sparked by one good idea today. In 1980, one idea led to 40 more ideas. The idea multiplier rose in the early 1990s, especially in the computer and telecommunications sectors. Five years later, during the late 1990s, we had the "New Economy," with soaring incomes and productivity growth.

Since 2005, the idea multiplier has been stuck at around 200:1. This stalling may help explain why productivity and innovation have stagnated since the Global Financial Crisis. A flat idea multiplier translates, all else equal, into slower growth. Today, the idea multiplier is rising again, unaffected by the trauma of COVID-19. The multiplier now stands at 400:1, double its level through most of the past two decades. This jump is not simply due to the Internet. We had that more than a decade ago. The idea multiplier is surging because the globalization of ideas is accelerating. Why? Because more ideas are coming from more parts of the world, leading to more ideas right back here in the United States.

According to calculations by me and my colleagues, the increase in international knowledge sharing since 1990 is responsible for more than *half* of all new scientific discoveries since that time. But there's more to the story than researchers from one country building upon knowledge of those from another country. International collaboration within research teams has also risen. The percentage of influential papers with authors in two or more countries has increased sevenfold since 1980, while the average distance between any two collaborators has more than doubled.[13] One surprising reason for the lengthening distance between research collaborators: an increase in collaboration of private-sector research between the United States and China.

WHERE THE IDEA MULTIPLIER IS STRONGEST

In the pharmaceutical industry, the idea multiplier is generating treatments such as the mRNA vaccines that ended the global COVID-19 pandemic. Researchers are exploring the use of mRNA technology, pioneered by Nobel laureates Drew Weissman and Katalin Karikó at the University of Pennsylvania, to treat cancer and rare genetic diseases.

And AI is driving advances in drug discovery, a slow and costly process. To bring a single new drug to market, a pharmaceuticals company might spend billions of dollars over a decade. More recently, however, Insilico Medicine used AI algorithms to identify a therapeutic candidate for pulmonary fibrosis in just 46 days. CAR-T cell therapy, a promising therapy for lymphoma and leukemia, reflects idea exchange among immunology, gene editing, and oncology, with collaboration among scientists from China, the United States, and Europe. It is now in more than 300 trials around the world to treat cancers that have been resistant to immunotherapy.

THE BIGGEST RISK TO GLOBALIZATION

A sharp rise in tariffs would be a short-term negative shock to growth. But the more important globalization trend we should care about is the trade in ideas. And by this measure, globalization is not slowing, but rather accelerating.

An increase in the global idea multiplier should serve as a tailwind in future productivity and growth. This dimension of globalization is one that too few talk about. While this dimension of globalization would seem to transcend the prospects or fall-out of tariffs on imported goods, the trade in ideas is not immune to geopolitical risk that could curtail the flow of knowledge across countries.

Chinese history reminds us that the flow of ideas and its spur to innovation can cease. Over the past 30 years, China has risen from an impoverished, agrarian economy into one of the world's economic and research powers. Yet I sometimes forget that China's rise is a case of "back to the future." Centuries ago, China—not the West—was the world's economic and technological leader.

Imagine that you're a spice trader on the coast of Africa in the year 1415. A ship appears on the horizon. The ship is massive, as large as a modern aircraft carrier, but made of wood—nine masts and 1,000 sailors. The ship blocks out the sun, casting you in shadow. And then you see 60 more of these ships and, behind those, 200 smaller ships.

That fleet, as legend has it, belonged to Chinese Admiral Zheng He, who led expeditions to Africa, India, and Indonesia long before Christopher Columbus set sail for America. Some believe that his fleet was larger than the entire British Navy. But within 70 years, that fleet disappeared.

The Ming Dynasty outlawed ocean vessels and turned inward. No more exchange of knowledge, the start of China's 500-year decline.

A present-day example shows the power of globalization, including those nations that close themselves to the free exchange of scientific and cultural knowledge. Figure 3.4 shows a nighttime satellite image of East Asia, one of the most vibrant centers of global commerce over the past few decades. Notice North Korea. No lights at night. No growth. North Korea has access to the Internet, but not unfettered access to ideas. It's not just the technology that explains innovation. It's the exchange of ideas that helps drive it.

Figure 3.4   North Korea is an island of economic darkness, cut off from the free exchange of ideas.
Source: Wikimedia

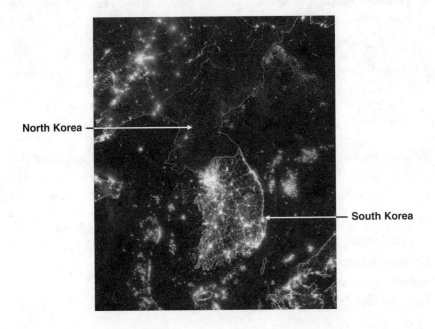

NOTES

1. Barboza, D. (2016). "How China Built 'IPhone City' with Billions in Perks for Apple's Partner." *The New York Times*, December 29, 2016. https://www .nytimes.com/2016/12/29/technology/apple-iphone-china-foxconn.html.

2. "White." (2024). Llnl.gov. Advanced Simulation and Computing. 2024. https:// asc.llnl.gov/computers/historic-decommissioned-machines/white.

3. "iPhone 15 Plus." (2024). Apple. 2024. https://www.apple.com/shop/buy-iphone/ iphone-15?afid=p238%7Cs84Fox0Ge-dc_mtid_20925d2q39172_ pcrid_705483176152_pgrid_154285222318_pntwk_g_pchan__pexid__ptid_ kwd-984596472683_&cid=wwa-us-kwgo-iphonc-slid—NonCorc-iPhone15-.

4. Friedman, T. L. (2007). *The World Is Flat: Brief History of the Twenty-First Century.* New York: Picador. Pages 516–517.

5. Goodhart, C. A. E., and Pradham, M. J. (2020). *The Great Demographic Reversal: Ageing Societies, Waning Inequality, and an Inflation Revival.* Cham, Switzerland: Palgrave Macmillan.

6. Contrary to conventional wisdom, the sharp rise in tariff rates and other protectionist measures were not a primary cause of the Great Depression. For many countries during the early 1930s, a bigger headwind was the gold standard, which limited the flexibility of monetary policymakers to boost demand. For more details, see the excellent 2009 paper *The Slide to Protectionism in the Great Depression: Who Succumbed and Why?* by Doug Irwin and Barry Eichengreen (NBER WP#15142).

7. According to the Megatrends Model GDP growth and stock returns have been somewhat higher due to globalization, while domestic rates of investment have been reduced, especially in manufacturing over the past several decades. I do not want to imply that I am against "free trade." Rather, I am rather pointing out that there is a more important dimension of globalization in an increasingly service-based economy that has less to do with cargo ships and more to do with the dissemination of knowledge. For a deeper discussion on the nuances of global trade, I suggest Dani Rodrick's 2017 book, *Straight Talk on Trade.*

8. Some of this section is adapted from Vanguard research papers I wrote with some colleagues, including *The Idea Multiplier* (Davis, et al., 2020) and *How America Innovates* (2022).

9. See also the discussion beginning on page 49 in Azhar, Azeem. (2021). *The Exponential Age: How Accelerating Technology Is Transforming Business, Politics, and Society.* New York, NY: Diversion Books.

10. Adams, J. D. (1990). "Fundamental Stocks of Knowledge and Productivity Growth," *Journal of Political Economy,* 98(4), 673–702. https://doi.org/10.1086/261702.

11. Stringfellow, E. (2020). "Reading This on Your Smartphone? Thank Hedy Lamarr!" MassBio. March 30, 2020. https://www.massbio.org/news/recent-news/reading-this-on-your-smartphone-thank-hedy-lamarr/.

12. De Best, Raynor. (2024). "PayPal: Statistics and Facts." www.statista.com. December 10, 2024. https://www.statista.com/topics/2411/paypal/.

13. I define influential ideas as the 10,000 most cited at any time.

CHAPTER FOUR

NOT DESTINY, JUST DEMOGRAPHICS

THE BIRTH OF THE FIRST BABY BOOMER

On January 1, 1946, at one second past midnight, Kathleen Casey entered the world at Philadelphia's St. Agnes Hospital. Weighing 7 pounds, 5 ounces, she was the daughter of a Navy machinist's mate and his home-maker wife. Her birth marked the beginning of a demographic shift. Kathleen Casey, later Kathleen Casey-Kirschling, was America's first "Baby Boomer."[1]

In the months that followed, maternity wards across the country filled up at an unprecedented rate. Births in the United States surged 50% from January to October 1946. By the end of the 1940s, 32 million babies had been born, compared with just 24 million in the 1930s. The baby boom was so significant that it reversed a multi-decade decline in U.S. birth rates due to the Great Depression.

Over the years, Casey-Kirschling embodied the Baby Boomer experience. She went from student to worker, parent to retiree. Fittingly, she became the first Baby Boomer to receive Social Security benefits in February 2008 at age 62.[2] Her life's transitions mirrored those of many Baby Boomers, the generation that has reshaped U.S. society and its demographic composition over the past 75 years.

DEMOGRAPHICS IS NOT DESTINY

Today, as Baby Boomers like Casey-Kirschling leave the labor force in droves, some experts warn of slower economic growth, higher inflation, and increased fiscal strain. Their logic is simple: slower labor force growth will hamper economic output, while a rising population of older Americans will boost demand for healthcare and social services, pressuring government budgets.

However, demographics is not destiny. It can be a factor, but it's not fate. The U.S. economy is a complex ecosystem of forces that extend beyond population size. While demographics can affect economic outcomes, other megatrends like technology and fiscal policy often exert a far larger influence.

Consider the experience of major economies over the past 200 years. The fact is that nations with slowing population growth have been as likely to experience *accelerating* economic growth (52% of the cases) as they have been to witness slower growth (48% of the cases). Inflation trends are equally split, with no clear causal relationship between population changes today and price increases tomorrow. If demographic shifts were truly destiny, the patterns in Figure 4.1 wouldn't look like a 50-50 coin toss.

Figure 4.1   The relationship between population growth and economic outcomes is a coin toss.

Note: The charts analyze instances where population growth slowed, comparing GDP growth and inflation outcomes. The sample includes data from 1800 to 1960 for G7 countries and from 1960 to 2022 for 150 other countries. "Similar" outcomes are defined as differences within +/− 0.5 percentage points in GDP or CPI growth compared to the previous decade.

In **52%** of instances, economies were able to deliver stronger or similar growth despite slowing population growth.

In **53%** of instances, inflation was lower when population growth was slowing.

DEMOGRAPHICS: TWO DIMENSIONS

Demographics, a science pioneered by London haberdasher John Gaunt in his book *Natural and Political Observations Made upon the Bills of Mortality* (1691), describes a population's growth rate, age, gender, race, religion, income, and any number of other defining characteristics. This chapter focuses on two particular dimensions of U.S. demographics: (1) population growth, and (2) the number of older Americans.

Since the birth of the last of the Baby Boomers in 1964, the U.S. population has grown more slowly. The primary reasons are rising levels of wealth and education that tend to lower fertility rates. The population has also become older as people have fewer children and longevity (life expectancy) increases. But these changes are nothing new. In the United States, a relatively young country, population growth has slowed and life expectancy has increased for most of the past 100 years (Figure 4.2). The Baby Boomer generation was an exception to this longer running trend.

Figure 4.2   The relationship between demographics and inflation is weak.

This figure shows how demographic change has had little impact on inflation. Other forces like monetary and fiscal policy and technology play a much larger role.

Note: The figure shows the historical contribution of demographics to the deviation of inflation from its long-run average, between 1890 and 2023, contrasting this with all other drivers (aggregated) in the grey color. Other drivers include other megatrends, cyclical factors and monetary policy. Figure shows inflation since 1960 for greater clarity.

Source: Author's calculations, as of May 2024.

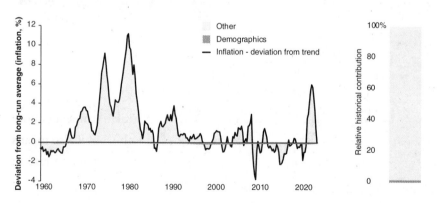

POPULATION GROWTH AND THE ECONOMY: THREE FACTS

When the Baby Boomers were born, Stanford University biologist Paul Ehrlich predicted that the population surge would result in a social and economic collapse, an echo of Thomas Malthus' misguided predictions two centuries earlier in *An Essay of the Principle of Population* (1798). Ehrlich's 1968 book *The Population Bomb* forecast rising commodity prices and resource depletion. Ehrlich made an infamous bet with economist Julian Simon that from 1980 to 1990, population growth would raise the prices of five basic commodities used in industrial production: chromium, copper, nickel, tin, and tungsten. Simon took the other side of that bet, assuming that technological advances would make minerals more plentiful. Simon won the bet. Prices fell.

This cautionary tale underscores the flawed logic of "demographics is destiny." The following are three more accurate depictions about population growth and its economic effects.

Fact #1: Population Growth Does Not Drive Inflation

Every new worker is also a consumer. A rising population means more people making products and providing services (supply), but it also means more people buying them (demand). When supply and demand rise in tandem, prices should not change. This logic extends in both directions. Slower population growth means fewer producers, but it also means fewer consumers. Inflation fears tied to demographics overlook this crucial offsetting effect.

Consider the Baby Boomers again. Between 1964 and 1982, as additional 39 million Boomers entered the workforce, labor force participation rose from 58 to 64%, a surge equivalent to California's current population. Women's participation jumped even more, from 38 to 53%. According to the "demographics is destiny" view, this surge in the workforce should have driven prices down. But the opposite happened. Inflation soared, peaking at over 13% in 1980. But it wasn't demographics that caused the Great Inflation (indeed, if demographics drove inflation, we should have had the "Great Deflation"). Rather, the Great Inflation was the result of energy-supply shocks, fiscal deficits, and policy mistakes by the U.S. Federal Reserve, as we'll see later.

The causal relationship running from demographics to inflation is weak. If you seek more proof, Figure 4.2, derived from our megatrends framework, shows the contributions of demographics to inflation since 1890. Even if you squint hard, you won't find much cause and effect. Over the past 100 years, demographics have accounted for less than 2% of the total volatility (i.e., ups and downs) in the inflation rate. The same will be true in the decades ahead.

Fact #2: GDP Growth Is Driven by Technology, Not Population Growth

It's intuitive to think that more people translate into more GDP, all else equal. But our megatrends analysis reveals that all else is rarely ever equal. Over the past century and more, the biggest driver of GDP has been *technology in the form of machines that may automate our work and those that complement human skills and talents.* To demonstrate technology's importance, Figure 4.3 compares rolling 10-year changes in real GDP growth, population growth, and productivity growth (i.e., "technology") for the United Kingdom (Panel A) and the United States (Panel B) since 1900. The pattern is striking. Real GDP growth tracks productivity, not population growth. The correlation

Figure 4.3   GDP follows technology, not demographics.

These charts show the 10-year rolling changes in demographics (population growth), technology (productivity growth) and GDP in the United Kingdom (Panel A) and the United States (Panel B) from 1900 to present.

Note: Demographics represents rolling 10-year average annualized growth in population. Technology represents rolling 10-year average annualized growth in real GDP per capita, a proxy for productivity growth. Of course, other factors can influence productivity growth including education. The Real GDP line is the sum in population growth and productivity growth, or GDP = Demographics + Technology. Scale in U.S. figure truncated during WWII for visual clarity.

Source: Author's calculations from Bank of England, U.S. Census Bureau, and FRED databases.

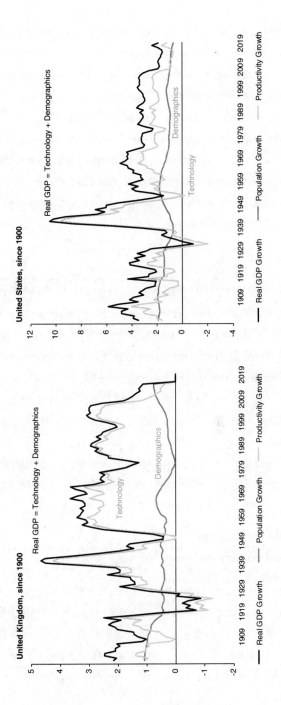

between GDP growth and productivity growth is 97%, while the correlation to population growth is a mere 7%. For economic growth, technology dominates demographics in importance by a wide margin.

Take the Industrial Revolution as an example. The U.K.'s population grew steadily, but its economy surged only after technological advances like steam engines for power and mechanized looms for textiles boosted efficiency and growth. If demographics were truly destiny, the United Kingdom would have experienced steady GDP growth alongside population growth. Instead, it surged when productivity surged.[3]

Fact #3: Extreme Demographic Change Can Tip the Scales

While normal shifts in population have limited effects, extreme shifts can dwarf the impact of technology. When demographics and technology push and pull in opposite directions, the demographic swings need to be exceptionally pronounced to dominate GDP.

Looking ahead, the United States is unlikely to experience such a major drag, as the anticipated changes in population growth rates are not large. Between 2030 and 2040, for instance, the U.S. Census Bureau anticipates annualized population growth of 0.5%, modestly lower than the 0.7% annualized growth rate between 2010 and 2020.

But a more pessimistic reality may unfold in China. Its "one-child policy" (1979–2016) significantly reduced population growth. China's working-age population is now shrinking, while the over-65 population is surging. Unlike the United States, which has relied on immigration to bolster population growth, China has not. Projections from the United Nations suggest that China's population could decline by 780 million people in 2100 (see Figure 4.4). That anticipated change is dramatic, representing a population decline larger than twice the current U.S. population.[4] Yes, China will lose population amounting to the size of two present-day Americas by the year 2100.

Figure 4.4   AI is unlikely to offset China's population decline.
This chart shows China's projected population change from 2024 to 2100, with a sharp decline beginning in the 2030s.

SOURCE: U.N. World Population Prospects 2024

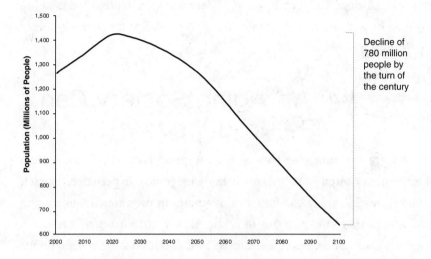

To increase or even maintain economic output, China would need to capitalize on technological improvements *four times as large* as those experienced in the United Kingdom during the Industrial Revolution. (You may want to read that sentence again). AI shows some promise, but virtually none of our simulations shows a labor-saving effect that high. This is the primary reason why my evaluation of China's long-term economic prospects beyond 2040 is not rosy. China's lack of immigration appears to be a more limiting factor that even the more extreme version of AI transformation may not be able to reverse. By 2040, China's level of GDP is unlikely to catch up to the United States despite its having a much larger population.[5]

TWO FACTS ABOUT AGING

While the size of a population matters, so too does its age. But again, conventional wisdom can get it wrong. Here are two truths about aging informed by the megatrends framework that challenge the "demographics is destiny" narrative.

Fact #4: An Aging Society Can Be Productive

The concept that an aging society is an unproductive one is overstated. Older workers often have the most knowledge and experience. In fact, studies show that aging encourages investment in productivity enhancing technologies that in turn result in economic growth.[6] Academic research by Acemoglu and Restrepo, for example, find a relationship between population age and an economy's use of industrial robots. In 2014, U.S. manufacturers used 9.1 robots for every 1,000 workers. Germany and Japan, with older populations, have higher adoption of industrial robots. Japanese manufacturers used 14.2 robots for every 1,000 workers. Their German counterparts used 17.0. Once again, changes in technology and its adoption drive more of the change in economic growth than demographics. But technology isn't the only driver of changes in productivity.

Older Americans are also working longer. According to the Pew Research Center, nearly one in five workers aged 65+ was employed in 2023.[7] That percentage is expected to growth meaningfully over the coming decade for several reasons, including the improved education and health of this older population compared to past generations. Another factor at play is the U.S. labor market's gravitation toward more "age-friendly" jobs as the percentage of the labor force working in more physically demanding occupations has declined.[8]

As older workers stay in the workforce longer, an aging population is likely to be a smaller drag on growth than the "demographics is destiny" view implies. And if AI augments and automates more tasks, AI-related technology could offset a decent share of the remaining Baby Boomer retirements expected by the end of this decade. (We discussed this in Chapter 2).

Fact #5: Older People Do Not Spend Less—They Spend Differently

Aging doesn't automatically make people spend less, although it does change what they spend on. According to consumer spending data gathered across many developed economies, spending does not fall as people age. Figure 4.5 illustrates that an average consumer's spending, as a percentage of prime-age working income, remains somewhat flat after age 30.

Figure 4.5   Our lifetime level of consumption tends to remain constant, even after retirement.

Source: Vanguard analysis, based on data from U.N. National Transfer Accounts

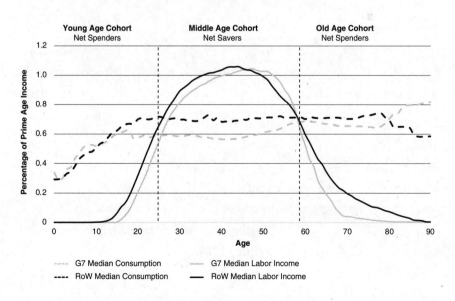

But as one ages, the spending mix shifts. For instance, older consumers may demand more services such as healthcare and fewer goods such as baby buggies or video game consoles (though beating my college-aged kids in video games remains my guilty pleasure). For inflation, this means that aging is unlikely to affect the general level of prices. Some products may go up in price, but others may fall. These changes in prices tend to offset each other, much as an additional worker and an additional consumer offset impacts on supply and demand. A society's changing age profile can raise or lower prices for different demographic groups, but its impact on the general price level has empirically been modest.

DEMOGRAPHICS IS NOT DESTINY

The concept of "demographics is destiny" traces back to nineteenth-century French philosopher Auguste Comte. But after 200 years of evidence, it's clear that Comte's axiom is flawed. Demographics matters, but it is a force that is part of a much larger dynamic system. To best assess our economic and investment future, we need to look holistically at technology, fiscal policy, globalization, and demographics. Demographics alone won't tell us if inflation and interest rates will rise or if GDP and stocks will fall. Demographic change will likely affect specific sectors, particularly health care, and may apply pressure on federal budgets, but it won't predetermine the fate of the U.S. economy.

Demographics is not destiny. It's just demographics.

NOTES

1. Jones, L. (2006). "The First Baby Boomer Turns 60." Lanny Jones. 2006. https://www.lannyjones.com/the-first-baby-boomer-turns-60/.
2. Lassiter, M. (2008). "Nation's First Baby Boomer Receives Her First Social Security Retirement Benefit." SSA Press Office. Social Security Administration. February 12, 2008. https://www.ssa.gov/pressoffice/pr/babyboomer-firstcheck-pr.pdf.
3. Another interesting historical fact on this topic that one could work into a dinner party conversation to impress your friends and colleagues: Population growth slowed during some of the greatest periods of cultural and technological change in human history, including (1) the Industrial Revolution, (2) the Enlightenment, (3) the Renaissance, and (4) in the United States more recently, the Roaring 1920s. This statement is based off of calculations made from annual or interpolated decennial data accessed through Global Financial Data.
4. According to the U.S. Census Bureau, the current U.S. population is approximately 335 million.
5. For more on China's economic future, please see Vanguard's annual economic and market outlook and related commentary at https://corporate.vanguard.com/content/dam/corp/research/pdf/isg_vemo_2025.pdf.
6. Acemoglu and Restrepo (2017). "Robots and Jobs: Evidence from US Labor Markets." National Bureau of Economic Research Working Paper Series, 23 Mar. 2017, www.nber.org/papers/w23285.
7. https://www.pewresearch.org/social-trends/2023/12/14/the-growth-of-the-older-workforce/.
8. See for instance the 2022 NBER working paper entitled "The Rise of Age-Friendly Jobs" at https://www.nber.org/papers/w30463.

CHAPTER FIVE

GOVERNMENT DEBT AND DEFICITS: ONE MATTERS MORE

THE CHECK THAT CHANGED AMERICA

On January 31, 1940, Ida May Fuller, a 65-year-old retired legal secretary from Ludlow, Vermont, opened her mailbox to find something historic: the first monthly Social Security check ever issued (Figure 5.1). It was for $22.54—not much by today's standard, but it marked the beginning of a shift.[1]

Figure 5.1   Ida May Fuller receives the first monthly Social Security check.

Source: USA Today

President Franklin D. Roosevelt had signed the Social Security Act into law in 1935, creating a program that has become the foundation of the U.S. retirement system. The program also created an explicit link between the age distribution of the U.S. population and the federal budget. At the program's inception, this link was barely perceptible. By the end of 1940, only 220,000 Americans, less than 1% of the population, had received benefits totaling about $35 million—a rounding error on the government's balance sheet.

Today, this link is a powerful driver of federal spending. Some 70 million Americans, 20% of the population, benefit from more generous Social Security payments, with annual adjustments for inflation. And since 1965, Ida May Fuller's younger counterparts have qualified for Medicare, government-financed healthcare benefits.[2] In 2024, government spending on healthcare benefits and Social Security payments amounted to more than $2.5 trillion, a figure that exceeds 10% of GDP.

These programs have significantly reduced poverty among the elderly. For instance, without Social Security, the poverty rate for seniors would be nearly 40%.[3] Millions of Americans now have much greater financial security in retirement. A much larger portion of the U.S. population are now able to access healthcare, too. In 1963, less than 60% of Americans aged 65 and older had health insurance. And these policies typically provided limited coverage. An illness or, more simply, the march of time and the attendant need for healthcare could spell financial ruin.[4]

But today almost all older Americans benefit from Medicare. This change began on June 30, 1965, when President Lyndon B. Johnson presented former shopkeeper and President Harry Truman with the first Medicare card at Truman's Presidential Library in Independence, Missouri. Americans are now protected, at least to some extent, from rising healthcare bills as they age.[5]

But make no mistake. These programs are expensive—and only becoming more so as America ages. This raises a fundamental question: *what are the implications of rising U.S. government debt levels?*

THE DEBT MOUNTAIN: A BALANCED VIEW

Figure 5.2 illustrates the U.S. debt-to-GDP ratio over the past 235 years. For most of American history, the government's debt was manageable, only surging during major crises like the Civil War, the Great Depression, and World War II. After World War II (WWII), debt dropped sharply as the

Figure 5.2 The U.S. debt-to-GDP ratio has varied since the nation's founding.

Source: Congressional Budget Office and Vanguard, as of February 2024

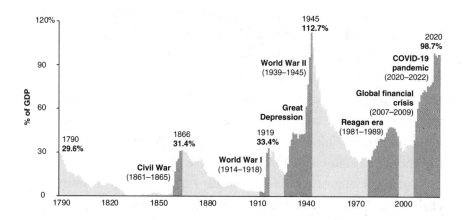

economy boomed and deficits shrank, falling to below 30% of GDP by 1970. However, in the following decades, debt rose again due to entitlement spending **on government programs like Social Security and Medicare**, tax reforms, and recent crises like the Global Financial Crisis (GFC) and COVID-19. By 2024, U.S. debt had reached nearly 100% of GDP—the highest since WWII. At present, U.S. government debt outstanding is $35 trillion.

But focusing solely on the debt-to-GDP ratio can be misleading. Imagine judging a household's financial health by its credit card balance alone. It's not just the balance that matters, but the household's income, job situation, and future earnings potential. For governments, the same logic applies. Debt must be viewed alongside temporary developments (like borrowing for recessions and wars) and longer-term growth trends.

This chapter explains why debt discussions are often misunderstood. Simply put, there are three key elements that matter for fiscal health: (1) the government budget, (2) demographics, and (3) technology. This straightforward framework should help us assess multidimensional fiscal health in the past and in the future.

The four conclusions are as follows: First, the level of debt is less important than the evolution of *structural fiscal deficits*, which arise from recurring imbalances between spending and taxation. Second, these structural deficits are a recent phenomenon, largely due to entitlement spending as society ages. Third, there seems to be a growing complacency surrounding U.S. fiscal health. Today, that health is increasingly fragile given the combination of a growing imbalance between tax revenues and spending, tied to aging, and poor trends in innovation that have boosted GDP. Fourth, an improvement in the future along either of these fronts would reduce the potential headwinds from rising structural deficits that could "crowd out" growth. Bipartisan fiscal reform would be the most assured way to increase America's odds for future economic and financial success.

WHY DEBT-TO-GDP IS A FLAWED MEASURE

A common belief is that once debt exceeds a certain level, poor economic growth and inflation soon follow. In their 2011 book *This Time Is Different: Three Centuries of Financial Folly*, Carmen Reinhart and Kenneth Rogoff warn of the negative effects when countries debt levels exceed 90% of GDP. But the historical record tells a more nuanced story, as one can see in Figure 5.3. It is not uncommon for economies to deliver strong growth despite relatively high levels of debt. In fact, the odds of an economy growing faster or more slowly once reaching 90% debt-to-GDP ratio are close to a coin toss.

Consider post-WWII America. Debt topped 110% of GDP in 1945, yet the U.S. experienced decades of robust growth driven by urbanization and technological innovation. Similar cases occurred in Belgium in the 1980s and Italy and Canada in the 1990s. The patterns are similar for future inflation, too.

Figure 5.3 makes the simple point that focusing solely on the debt/GDP ratio does not provide us with a reliable guidepost for the U.S. economic and financial outlook. Let me be clear: I do *not* intend to imply that debt is irrelevant (in fact, such an idea is dangerous). Rather, it means that we need a more nuanced metric of fiscal health.

Figure 5.3   Debt levels have a weak relationship with future economic performance.

In 64% of instances, economies were able to deliver stronger or similar growth despite high debt.

Slower growth
36% grew slower in the decade after debt/GDP exceeded 90%.

Higher or similar growth
64% grew at a faster or similar rate in the decade after debt/GDP exceeded 90%.

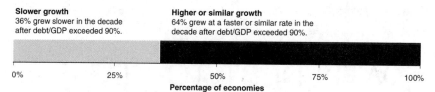

Notes: Sample includes only those observations where the debt-to-GDP ratio exceeds 90% at period t. Analysis compares the average annual GDP growth over the subsequent decade to the previous decade. The sample includes data from 1800 to 2022 for 150 countries. "Similar growth" contain those observations where differences were less than +/-0.5 percentage points.

In 44% of instances, inflation was higher or similar when debt was high.

Slower inflation
56% had lower inflation in the decade after debt/GDP exceeded 90%.

Higher or similar inflation
44% had higher or similar inflation in the decade after debt/GDP exceeded 90%.

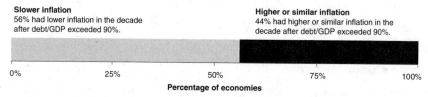

Notes: Sample includes only those observations where the debt-to-GDP ratio exceeds 90% at period t. Analysis compares the average annual CPI growth over the subsequent decade to the previous decade. The sample includes data from 1800 to 1960 for G7 countries (Canada, France, Germany, Italy, Japan, US, UK) and data from 1900 to 2022 for 150 countries. "Similar inflation" contain those observations where differences were less than +/-0.5 percentage points.

A SMARTER WAY TO MEASURE FISCAL HEALTH

Instead, the key variable is the *structural fiscal deficit*—the gap between government spending and tax revenues when growth is "normal." The structural deficit is illustrated by the dark-colored circle in Figure 5.4. The structural deficit is like a consumer's credit score—it reveals more about financial health than a single snapshot of debt. It adjusts for

Figure 5.4   For U.S. government deficits, the inner dark circle is what matters most. The dark circle represents the structural fiscal deficit and the factors that affect it.

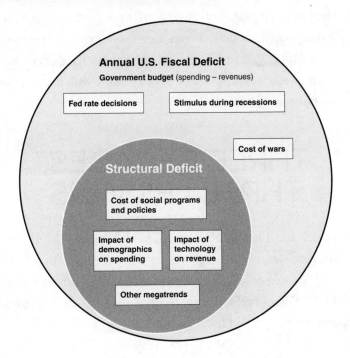

temporary factors like wars and recessions and can shift based on trends in demographics and technology.

Structural deficits provide a much clearer picture of fiscal health than debt/GDP ratios. In America's own history, the two concepts have often moved in different directions. At the end of World War II, the debt/GDP ratio exceeded 100%, but structural fiscal deficits were near zero. Why? Because government spending fell after the war, and taxes remained high. By contrast, in the 1970s, debt was low (around 30% of GDP), but structural deficits were high. These structural deficits contributed to the Great Inflation and surge in interest rates during the 1970s.

Structural deficits offer a more accurate guide for assessing fiscal sustainability. Structural deficits have been highly correlated at over 70% with inflation expectations and long-term U.S. Treasury bond yields. The lesson is that deficits can lead (and have led) to higher interest rates and borrowing costs under certain conditions, thus "crowding out" private sector growth. Debt levels, per se, don't do that. But rising structural deficits can if they are persistent. Our data-driven framework explicitly captures those conditions and finds that such instances are rare but have occurred in U.S. history. Again, we just need to know where to look with a framework that zeros in on cause and effect.

THREE DECADES, THREE LESSONS

Evaluating U.S. fiscal health of three different decades—the 1940s, 1970s, and 1990s—provides useful insights as to how our future fiscal health may involve. Each decade reveals how the combination of three megatrends—fiscal deficits, demographics, and technology—can have material and underappreciated effects on fiscal health.

The 1940s: Excellent Fiscal Health Amid High Debt

During WWII, deficits soared to finance the war effort. Annual deficits averaged nearly 20% from 1942 to 1945, with debt peaking at more than 110% of GDP. Despite record-high debt levels, the post-war decades produced economic prosperity; average American incomes rose by more than 50%, and government debt fell to below 40% of GDP by 1965.

How? The three megatrends of fiscal deficits, demographics, and technology all contributed to excellent fiscal health. The structural deficit was at times in surplus, thanks to reduced spending and high taxes. The Baby Boom produced 78 million new future taxpayers. Productivity growth, boosted by the transistor and early mainframe computers, further strengthened fiscal health.

The lesson? *Debt isn't destiny—it's the structural deficit that matters.*

The 1970s: Low Debt, but Poor Fiscal Health

On May 7, 1964, six months after he was elected U.S. President, Lyndon B. Johnson stood in front of a selection of students on Ohio University's College Green—a neatly cut quadrangle lawn at the heart of the Athens, OH campus. Half-way through his speech, he declared:

> *"There is in front of you young people today the promise of a greater tomorrow. It is a tomorrow that is brighter than yesterday ... and with your courage and with your compassion and your desire, we will build the Great Society. It is a Society where no child will go unfed, and no youngster will go unschooled. Where no man who wants work will fail to find it. Where no citizen will be barred from any door because of his birthplace or his color or his church."*

Two weeks later, in a speech at the University of Michigan, the President outlined his vision for "The Great Society," leading to major federal initiatives in civil rights, education, health care, and poverty reduction. This agenda echoed Franklin D. Roosevelt's New Deal. Programs like Medicare and Medicaid were introduced, tightening the link between federal spending and demographics, especially as the population aged and longevity increased.

The United States ran consistent fiscal deficits beginning in the late 1960s and throughout the 1970s. Those deficits were not solely the result of periodic, deep recessions and spending related to the Vietnam War. Although demographics at this time were favorable, the technological slowdown in the 1970s worsened overall fiscal health. (It turns out disco was not a GPT.)

Despite debt of just 30% of GDP, the 1970s were defined by stagflation. Inflation rose at a rate of more than 10% a year, leading to soaring borrowing costs. By December 1979, a 30-year mortgage rate sat at 12.9%. The Federal Reserve's loose policy of keeping interest rates too low was a major contributor to expectations of higher future inflation. But the Federal Reserve was not solely to blame for the Great Inflation of the 1970s. My framework reveals that structural deficits played a contributing role as well. Indeed, when we zero in on the cause and effect of the Great Inflation of the 1970s, this is what you find as the root causes:

- Monetary policy (i.e., Federal Reserve "too easy"): 48% of the Great Inflation
- Structural fiscal deficits (i.e., classic "crowding out" effect): 32% of the Great Inflation[6]
- All other factors (e.g., OPEC oil shocks, weak productivity): 20% of the Great Inflation

The two lessons?

- *Low debt doesn't guarantee strong fiscal health.*
- *Large, persistent structural deficits can crowd out and lower growth by raising borrowing costs, as they did during the 1970s.*[7]

The 1990s: Technology Boom Can Overcome Demographics-Driven Deficits

On the morning of September 29, 1999, Director of Federal Budget Issues at the U.S. General Accounting Office Paul L. Posner sat before the Committee on Ways and Means at the House of Representatives (see Figure 5.5). He was about to testify on a rather unusual concern that had gained traction over the previous six years under the Clinton administration: whether U.S.

Figure 5.5   This actually happened: An uncommon agenda topic in D.C.

SOURCE: The front page of Posner's testimony to Congress in September 1999.

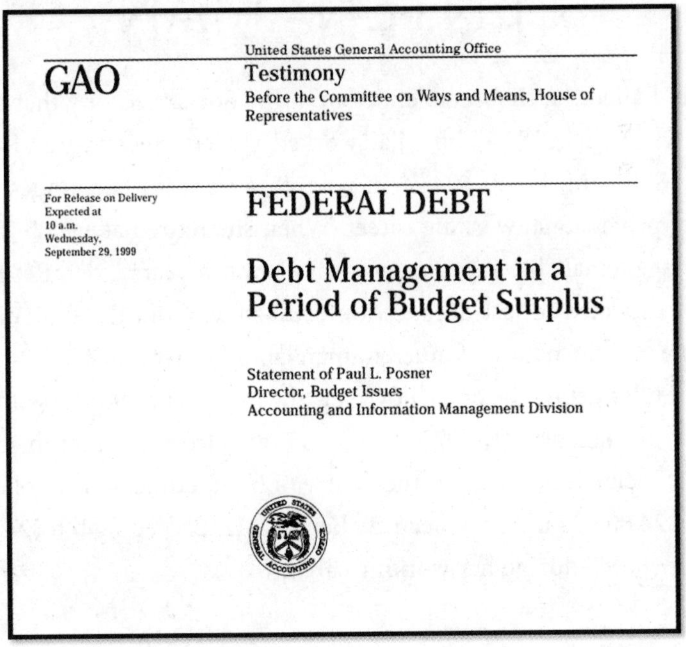

United States General Accounting Office

GAO

Testimony

Before the Committee on Ways and Means, House of Representatives

For Release on Delivery
Expected at
10 a.m.
Wednesday,
September 29, 1999

FEDERAL DEBT

Debt Management in a Period of Budget Surplus

Statement of Paul L. Posner
Director, Budget Issues
Accounting and Information Management Division

government debt was *too low* and was negatively impacting the economy and financial markets.

At that time, the Treasury was running a budget surplus of nearly 4% of GDP, bolstered by tax increases on income, corporate profits, gas, and Social Security benefits, along with reduced defense spending.[8]

This strong fiscal position was achieved despite slowing population growth and rising entitlement liabilities. Why? Fiscal health benefitted from a technology-fueled productivity boom led by the Internet. By the time Posner was testifying to Congress in 1999, federal debt had fallen from 48% in 1994 to 38% of GDP, with projections suggesting it could approach zero if current trends continued.

The lesson? *Technology booms can reduce structural deficits.*

SOCIAL SECURITY'S FIRST CENTENARIAN

Ida May Fuller, the first recipient of monthly Social Security that we met earlier, was born in 1874. Fuller had worked as a legal secretary and school-teacher. She contributed $24.75 in payroll taxes from her modest salary over her professional working career. When she retired at age 65 in 1939, the average female life expectancy was only a few years older. Retirement was not expected to last decades, unfortunately, given the limitations in medicine and the nature of much human labor at that time.[9]

Ida Fuller defied the odds, however. She lived to be 100 years old, passing away on January 31, 1975, exactly 35 years from the month she first received Social Security. Over the course of her lifetime, Fuller collected a total of $22,888.92 in Social Security benefits, far exceeding the $24.75 she had contributed during her working career.

Fuller's story exemplifies the long-term benefits, and long-term challenges, of Social Security and other government programs. These programs provide critical financial support for those who live significantly beyond the average life expectancy. In 1975, Fuller's story was a rare and extraordinary one. But given the evolving mix between the number of U.S. workers and retirees in the decades ahead, age-related deficits will continue to rise unless the megatrends of technology and deficits (e.g., government policy) shift in a meaningful way.

TWO POSSIBLE FUTURES

Today, the fiscal outlook is uncertain. Population growth is lower than it was in the 1990s, current productivity trends are weak, and entitlement spending is rising, now accounting for over 10% of GDP, up from 5% in the 1990s. Tax revenues have remained stable, between 15% and 20% of GDP, but structural deficits have increased over the past decade.

What our framework makes clear is that the 2030s will be shaped by a tug-of-war between technology and age-related structural deficits. Given the push and pull between these forces, two likely scenarios emerge (see Figure 5.6). And neither looks like the status quo.

Scenario (1): AI Buys Time (45–55% probability)

AI becomes a transformative technology, driving a productivity boom similar to the 1990s. Growth picks up and tax revenues rise during the 2030s. Federal debt rises, but at a slower pace, reaching 122% of GDP by 2040. Policymakers get some breathing room to consider fiscal reform, but I assume nothing is enacted during this period.

Scenario (2): AI Disappoints (30–40% probability)

AI fails to live up to expectations. Productivity remains stagnant, entitlement spending grows, and structural deficits climb. Interest rates rise in the 2030s as bond investors begin to demand higher yields on U.S. Treasury debt, which reaches 179% of GDP. Fiscal reform becomes unavoidable, but not before the U.S. economy faces higher inflationary pressures, slower growth, and the high likelihood of a fiscal-related recession from a spike in long-term interest rates tied to concerns over long-run fiscal sustainability.

Figure 5.6   The tug-of-war between technology and deficits will determine U.S. financial health.

SOURCE: Author's calculations

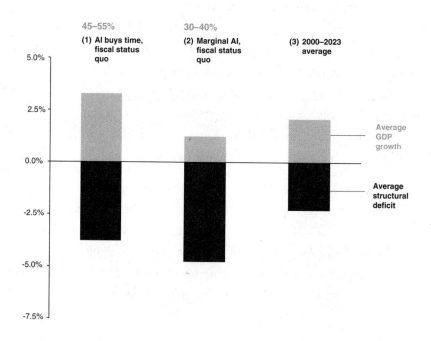

THE NATIONAL DEBT CLOCK AND THE 2030s

In 1989, Seymour Durst, a real estate developer, installed the now-famous National Debt Clock in midtown Manhattan. Back then, government debt had just exceeded $1 trillion. A 2018 *Washington Post* article profiled the history of the clock and its tally at the time of the story (see Figure 5.7). The *Washington Post* article ends by stating, "Even the National Debt Clock no longer gets quite the attention it once did. The clock has been moved to an alley off West 43rd Street where few pedestrians stop to look at it. On a recent summer evening, several Chinese tourists were the only ones taking photos of it."

Figure 5.7   The U.S. National Debt Clock in New York City, circa 1990s, ticks higher today.
Source: The Washington Post

The 2030s will present a pivotal moment—and a shift. If AI becomes a true general-purpose technology, the United States could experience a rare "best of both worlds" scenario: (1) robust economic growth, higher tax revenues, and narrowing structural reforms from the megatrends shift, *and* (2) a window for U.S. Congress to enact preemptive and even gradually phased-in fiscal reform. But if AI disappoints, the era of tough choices will arrive.

The clock is ticking. And the stakes are slowly rising.

NOTES

1. Earlier beneficiaries of the program, which had started in 1937, had received lump-sum payments.
2. https://www.archives.gov/milestone-documents/medicare-and-medicaid-act.
3. Social Security Lifts More People Above the Poverty Line Than Any Other Program, Center on Budget and Policy Priorities, cbpp.org.
4. https://www.ssa.gov/history/pdf/WhatMedicareMeant.pdf.
5. https://www.ssa.gov/history/lbjsm.html#:~:text=At%20the%20bill%2D signing%20ceremony,with%20the%20first%20Medicare%20card.
6. From a technical perspective, my framework finds empirical evidence consistent with the fiscal theory of the price level (Cochrane, J. J. (2023). The *Fiscal Theory of the Price Level.* Princeton University Press). When deficits are identified as structural, inflation expectations rise modestly all else equal, presumably under the belief that the fiscal authority (in this case, U.S. Congress) will not raise future tax rates or cut future government spending sufficiently to achieve long-run deficit sustainability.
7. In fact, my megatrends model finds only two significant incidents since 1890 where rising structural deficits in the U.S. led to a classic "crowding out" effect of raising inflation expectations and interest rates while lower GDP growth. The first was the late 1960s and 1970s (as discussed earlier) and, briefly, during part of COVID-19. It is noteworthy that both episodes were also accompanied by "easy" or too-lax monetary policy.
8. The Clinton administration was able to take advantage of the "peace dividend" following the collapse of the Soviet Union.
9. https://www.history.com/news/first-social-security-check.

100

CHAPTER SIX

MEGATRENDS AROUND THE WORLD

"OPEN YE GATES"

David Francis, president of the Saint Louis World's Fair, uttered those words on April 30, 1904. He was officially opening the World's Fair in celebration of the centennial of the 1803 Louisiana Purchase. That day, more than 200,000 visitors passed through the massive fairground's gates. They were eager to see exhibits from more than 50 countries showcasing the latest achievements in technology, machinery, science, and culture.

PALACE OF ELECTRICITY

Among the most popular exhibits at the 1904 Saint Louis World's Fair was the Palace of Electricity, a pentagon-shaped building that housed demonstrations on electricity's practical applications. Thomas Edison himself shared his inventions with the crowd, including the incandescent light bulb that had started electricity's J-curve. Inventors wowed visitors with early predecessors of the wireless cell phone and fax machine, sending "wireless telephony" messages across the fairgrounds without wires. An operable X-ray machine from Chicago was on display to signal electricity's potential in healthcare diagnosis and medical advances.

Leading technology companies of the era held cutting-edge applications of electricity in the palace. General Electric demonstrated early household appliances, while its electric lighting systems illuminated many parts of the fairgrounds at night. More than 100 other U.S. companies, including AT&T and Westinghouse, accounted for half the floor space at the Palace of Electricity. Part of this American dominance reflected location. The World Fair was being held in Saint Louis, a city far from the eastern seaboard cities of New York and Boston and an ocean away from the electrifying cities of London, Paris, and Berlin. U.S. companies had home-field advantage.

But there was more at work than just location. At the time, the U.S. economy was beginning to harness electricity faster than other countries. In his 1983 book *Networks of Power: Electrification in Western Society, 1880–1930*, author Thomas P. Hughes demonstrates how major electric power utilities in the United States focused on supplying the most heavily populated and industrialized urban centers, best clearing the way for electricity's adoption at times quicker than even the leading economies in Europe, including Great Britain.

ONE TECHNOLOGY, SIX COUNTRIES

America was not the only country with exhibits in the Palace of Electricity. Twelve other nations had displays. Yet only five were of such significance that they were highlighted for visitors in the 1904 Saint Louis World's Fair program guide—Germany, Great Britain, France, Italy, and Japan.[1]

At the fair, each of these countries stood out in demonstrating the commercial application of electricity for industry and manufacturing. Germany had among the largest number of exhibits, displaying commercial applications in chemicals, metallurgy (steel), and scientific instruments. Like the United States, Japan was rapidly industrializing in a period now known as the Meiji Restoration (1868–1912). Other large economies of the time, including China, Russia, and India, were notably absent from the Palace of Electricity. These countries had not one display, not one representative on this transformative technology.

WRITING ON THE WALL

World fairs and trade shows are an imperfect, fuzzy lens into an economy's relative standing in the world. Such events can be a mixture of hype and reality. We all know that no single factor determines a country's long-run economic development. Rather, it is a complex web of megatrends, institutions, and other factors that influence a country's performance over time. An economy's ability to effectively harness technology—a function of entrepreneurship, education, investment capital, government policy, and a multitude of other factors—comes into play.

The 1904 World Fair was but a snapshot in time of how some economies were beginning to harness the century's most transformative technology. Back then, electricity was still in the infancy of its J-curve. Nevertheless, in the days before the Internet and air travel, the World's Fair was a glimpse into the early twentieth century's future. The World's Fair was an environment where the Idea Multiplier thrived.

Over the next 20 years, the economies of the United States, United Kingdom, Germany, France, and Japan would continue to advance, with their collective growth outpacing many others. Individually, these nations would compete, sometimes in violent ways. But from an economic perspective, some of the writing was on the wall of Saint Louis's Palace of Electricity in 1904. In the years to come, these economies would pull ahead. Technology was a factor in shaping the economic world order.

QUESTIONS TODAY— ABOUT TOMORROW

Today, we may wonder which countries will excel should AI continue to advance as a general-purpose technology. AI has the potential to dramatically transform work and industry. But which economies outside of the United States are best placed to benefit from AI? As was the case for Japan in 1904, are there new entrants who will increase their economic stature on the world stage? Some look to stronger GDP growth in select emerging markets in South America, Asia, and Africa given their favorable demographics of high fertility and a younger population. Yet we also know that demographics is not destiny.

Which countries, if any, will follow the path of relative decline that China and Russia did in the early twentieth century? Most economists offer little optimism for the largest economies of Europe and Japan, quick to point out the high debt levels of these countries. But as we've seen, debt alone is not destiny either. Will China succumb to demographics-driven stagnation, or will its investments in AI overcome those headwinds?

Answering these questions has global implications beyond GDP statistics and stock markets. Our megatrends framework provides some guidance and leading indicators. Technology will not raise or lower all boats equally. Let's now explore which of the world's largest economies may surprise us most.

A MEGATRENDS DASHBOARD

Table 6.1 is a simple dashboard for 10 large economies today that ranks them along the dimensions of the four megatrends: technology (specifically, AI), globalization, demographics, and fiscal dynamics. The goal of Table 6.1 is to paint a broad mosaic of the relative headwinds and tailwinds these economies will likely face through the lens of our framework. The source data underlying these rankings, which I have grouped qualitatively into buckets, come from leading credible sources.

For AI, we access the Global AI Vibrancy Tool (https://aiindex.stanford .edu/vibrancy) compiled and maintained by the Stanford Institute for Human-Centered Artificial Intelligence. This visual dataset is a treasure trove of key indicators measuring a country's AI ecosystem such as data on private investment, AI company startups, AI infrastructure, and research-paper influence, to name a few. AI research published and cited in technical journals and at IT conferences are a modern-day equivalent of the exhibits on electricity held at the 1904 World's Fair.

Our measure on globalization follows our discussion of the Idea Multiplier and illustrates its relative rank using my team's calculations across the field of AI. Fiscal dynamics represent a country's average of its projected primary and cyclically adjusted fiscal deficit or surplus by the year 2030 or so, an effective proxy for its structural fiscal deficit. These projections come from the International Monetary Fund. Demographic information on future population growth and the share of a country's population over the age of 65 years old are taken from the United Nations and the World Bank.

Table 6.1 Megatrends Dashboard

| Country | Technology | | | Globalization | Demographics | | Fiscal Dynamics |
	AI investment	AI companies	AI research	AI Idea Multiplier	Population growth	% Age 65 years old	Structural deficits
United States	Very strong	Very strong	Very strong	Very strong	Fair	Fair	High
China	Strong	Strong	Very strong	Very strong	Negative	Fair	Very High
Germany	Fair	Strong	Fair	Strong	Negative	High	Surplus / balanced
Japan	Lower	Fair	Lower	Lower	Negative	Very High	High
India	Fair	Fair	Very strong	Very strong	Strong	Low	High
United Kingdom	Strong	Strong	Strong	Strong	Fair	Fair	Fair
Brazil	Lower	Lower	Lower	Lower	Fair	Low	Surplus / balanced
Canada	Fair	Strong	Fair	Strong	Strong	Fair	Surplus / balanced
Australia	Lower	Fair	Fair	Strong	Strong	Fair	Surplus / balanced
South Korea	Fair	Fair	Fair	Strong	Negative	High	Surplus / balanced

Source: Author's calculations and rankings, based on data sources described in the text

106

TWO KEY TAKEAWAYS

Takeaway #1: The United States and China Presently Dominate the Field of AI

Table 6.1 should make clear the commanding lead that the economies of the United States and China have in the field of AI. The United States continues to dominate in the number of private companies being funded in the field (nearly 5,000 alone since 2020) and the private capital that is being invested. Even China trails by a wide margin along these dimensions. China's investments, however, tower over most other countries on the list.

But other dimensions are relevant besides pure investment dollars when it comes to technology adoption and enhancement. R&D can figure prominently too, such as measures of the volume and impact of AI researchers within a country. In the field of AI research and influential conference proceedings, China and India perform very strongly, another indication of deep expertise as the field evolves. Infrastructure, say in terms of supercomputers or compute speed, may also matter in the years ahead. I have compiled a weighted index of eight of these aggregate measures in Figure 6.1 using Stanford's Global AI Vibrancy Tool. The higher the score, the stronger a country's current AI capabilities along this mosaic of measures.

The conclusion from the sets of bars is clear. The United States and China have the strongest AI capabilities, by a wide margin. India shows up third, which to me appears to parallel Japan's showing at the 1904 World's Fair, at least along this narrow dimension. Since investments are measured in absolute dollars, these rankings will tend to favor larger economies (such as Germany and Japan) over smaller ones (such as Canada or Australia). When looked at on a per-person basis (not shown here), the United States,

Figure 6.1   A weighted index of AI vibrancy.

Source: Author's calculations using a subset of eight indicators in Stanford's Global AI Vibrancy Tool, which can be accessed at https://aiindex.stanford.edu/vibrancy

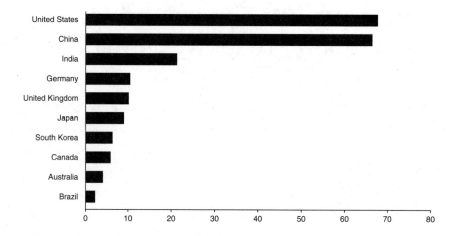

United Kingdom, Canada, and Australia remain in the top 15.[2] From the perspective of future global economic impact, size matters more than per-capita rankings.

Takeaway #2: Countries with Stronger Fiscal or Demographic Profiles Lag in AI, and Vice Versa

We know that demographics or fiscal dynamics, when viewed in isolation, can give an incomplete picture of an economy's health. Most notably, the United States and China share both a dominance in AI as well as the potential headwinds of structural deficits and an aging society. India possesses decent AI capabilities and robust population growth, although its fiscal dynamics are not strong.

The swing factor for many countries is likely to be along the dimension of globalization and the Idea Multiplier. Countries such as Canada and Australia are above average along the dimensions of demographics and fiscal deficits yet have lower direct AI investment. However, researchers and businesses in those countries show a high propensity in accessing (and contributing to) the growing domain of AI. This mosaic would suggest upside risk to not only these economies, but for the United Kingdom and South Korea as well.

Japan stands out with its combination of more significant fiscal and demographic headwinds along with lower ranks in terms of AI investments and the Idea Multiplier. For Japan and perhaps Germany, more AI investment would benefit future productivity growth given the demographic headwinds facing these economies. As is the case for the U.S. labor market, the potential for labor augmentation and automation is high for Japan and Europe given that the service sector accounts for roughly 80% of the workforce. The scope for potential benefits is high. But the clock will tick in coming years if such economies are to take fuller advantage of this potential.

FROM PHASE I TO PHASE II

As AI's J-curve advances in the years ahead as some expect, the technology's impact will move from Phase I (where investments are made but broader impact is more limited) to a more transformative Phase II, where adaption becomes widespread and where AI-based applications create new processes, services, and products. Phase II is when the J-curve turns positive.

At the 1904 Saint Louis World's Fair, electricity was still in Phase I, but the writing was on the wall for the economies that would win in Phase II.

The list remained the same from the 1900s through the Roaring 1920s. But that is not always the case.

The personal computer (PC) went through a similar journey, with Phase I involving the development of ever-cheaper workstations and desktop PCs. Computer calculations were faster, but they were not fundamentally new. Businesses and governments had been using bulkier mainframe computers for decades. The transition to Phase II occurred during the early 1990s with the development of PC software and operating systems that spawned an entire suite of business applications, from accounting spreadsheets to word processing. Paired with the Internet, time gave way to the New Economy of the 1990s.

Yet not all economies fully harnessed the transition from Phase I to Phase II. In fact, the world's technological leader of the 1980s did not because the PC's transformative power came in the form of software, not hardware. This story, worth noting as AI technology evolves, begins in 1983 in Las Vegas. This time, the real action was not at the casino.

"GEEK WEEK"

In November 1983, the world's largest computer trade show known as COMDEX took place at the Las Vegas Convention Center.[3] Affectionately known as "Geek Week" to computer aficionados, COMDEX had grown enormously since its first event in 1979. More than 1,400 computer companies, including leaders such as IBM and Apple, displayed their PC hardware products.[4] Microsoft displayed a prototype of its graphical user interface, which would go on sale two years later as Windows 1.0.

A 28-year-old gave a keynote address at COMDEX, touching upon the features of Microsoft's windowing software as his father advanced some slides on the overhead projector. The 28-year-old's name was Bill Gates.[5]

FROM JAPAN INC. TO SILICON VALLEY

At the time of the COMDEX computer show, Japan was the economic envy of the world. During the 1980s, Japan was the unquestioned technological superpower in electronics and related fields. Japan's economy boomed in the 1980s, with real GDP growth averaging well over 4% per year. Some leading experts worried about the relative decline of other leading markets, including the United States. An article in the March 11, 1985, issue of *Business Week* was titled "America's High Tech Crisis." A 1990 article in the *Harvard Business Review* suggested that Japanese IT companies would "dominate the 1990s" given their deep capabilities in electronics, including the fast-growing field for PC hardware.[6]

Yet the COMDEX computer trade shows in Las Vegas suggested that another type of technological change was coming—PC software. By the early 1990s, it would become apparent that technological leadership would shift from Phase I's PC hardware and mainframes to Phase II's PC software, an area where Japanese technology companies lagged. At the very moment that some books were claiming that the twenty-first century would "belong to Japan," the writing was on the wall that Japan's economic dominance could be challenged.

Glimpses of the United States' future prominence in computer technology and PC software during the 1990s could already be seen on the exhibit floors at the COMDEX trade show. By 2000 Japan's economic dominance had waned for several reasons. The most notable, to be sure, was a chronically weak banking system impaired from the 1989 stock market and real estate bubble. As noted by researchers Takeo Hoshi and Anil Kashyap, the lack of restructuring in the Japanese banking system following the 1989 bubble kept alive insolvent companies (which they refer to as "zombies"), making it more difficult for new, profitable companies to enter the market and compete.[7]

Yet often ignored in the conversation of Japan's multiple lost decades is its inability to maintain its leadership position in computer-based technology, a contributor to its poor rates of productivity growth. According to a 2010 NBER paper, the rise of software-based innovation led to the decline of Japan's IT industry and the resurgence of Silicon Valley. Japanese IT companies were 40% more productive than their U.S. counterparts in the mid-1980s, during the heart of Phase I of the PC. Yet by the mid-1990s, during the PC's Phase II, they were 60% *less* productive.[8] The lead had switched 180 degrees. In the 1998 book *Asia's Computer Challenge*, experts Jason Dedrick and Kenneth Kraemer put it more bluntly: "While the Japanese hardware industry had had mixed success in the PC era, the software industry has been an almost unqualified failure."[9]

Japan's stumble from Phase I to Phase II during the PC and Internet revolution was not the primary cause of its economic malaise. Factors involving both structural forces and structural reform played a role. But this reversal of fortunes certainly did not help.

WHAT THE UNITED STATES AND CHINA HAVE IN COMMON

Fast-forward to today, and the world's two largest economies—the United States and China—differ along several important dimensions. Yet these two powers share some important similarities. Both countries possess deep and growing leadership positions in AI. Our AI metrics reveal that no other countries come close to the depth and expertise that the technology companies in these countries currently possess. This should set up both economies well as AI moves from Phase I to Phase II. Nevertheless, both China and the United States must also contend with an aging population and growing levels of public debt. How AI's future J-curve compares to the headwinds of demographics and deficits is *the* critical question for every country. This is precisely the question our Megatrends Model is built to help answer.

AI AND SHIFTS AROUND THE WORLD

Today, megatrend signals are shifting yet again. As will be the case in the United States, the tectonic plates of the megatrends will produce meaningful shifts in the rest of the world by 2035. Several economies should surprise on the upside over the coming decade according to our megatrends scorecard. The list is a heterogenous mix of developed and emerging markets, a picture that a demographics-only lens would miss. The United Kingdom, Canada, Germany, India, and Singapore top the list of upside-surprise candidates. Conversely, Brazil, parts of Europe, and Japan could struggle unless investment increases meaningfully.

But let's make no mistake that the economic dominance of the United States and China is likely to continue for the foreseeable future. More than perhaps any other factor, AI's future J-curve will help shape the economic trajectories of both China and the United States in the coming decade. But in what way? Chapter 7 presents the U.S. economic outlook for the next decade or so.

Hollywood's first red-carpet movie premiere hints at how our story is likely to unfold.

NOTES

1. This is based on exhibits for Department F-Electricity, in the 1904 World Fair program. *Official catalogue of exhibitors. Universal exposition*. St. Louis, U.S.A. 1904. Document visual can be accessed at https://archive.org/details/official catalogu00loui/page/n755/mode/1up.

2. Other smaller countries that excel in our per-person AI Vibrancy Index include Singapore, Luxembourg, Israel, the United Arab Emirates, and Sweden.

3. COMDEX stood for **COM**puter **D**ealers' **EX**hibition.

4. See https://www.washingtonpost.com/archive/business/1983/11/29/computer-show-opens-in-las-vegas/c2d9919f-07b9-4a0f-97a5-77f3ec706fb7.

5. See https://www.seattlepi.com/business/article/83-comdex-saw-future-through-windows-1129900.php.

6. See https://hbr.org/1990/07/computers-and-the-coming-of-the-us-keiretsu.

7. Hoshi, T. and Kashyap, A. K. (2004). Japan's Financial Crisis and Economic Stagnation. *Journal of Economic Perspectives*, 18(1), 3–26.

8. See NBER Working Paper #16156 (2010) by Ashish Arora, Lee G. Branstetter, and Matej Drev.

9. Dedrick, J. and Kraemer, K. L. (1998). *Asia's Computer Challenge: Threat or Opportunity for the United States & the World?* New York: Oxford University Press.

CHAPTER SEVEN

THE TUG-OF-WAR: AI vs. FISCAL DEFICITS

HOLLYWOOD'S FIRST RED-CARPET PREMIERE

On October 18, 1922, movie stars Douglas Fairbanks and Enid Bennett strolled down a red carpet on Hollywood Boulevard into the grand court-yard of the Egyptian Theater for the premiere of *Robin Hood*. Crowds gathered. Cameras flashed. Inside, a live orchestra played under the glow of a dazzling sunburst ceiling, a tribute to the Egyptian sun god, Ra.

"The floodlights of filmdom turned the night into brilliance brighter than noonday," the *Hollywood Daily Citizen* reported. The *Los Angeles Times* declared it "a night of nights" signaling "a new epoch in the picture art."[1] This wasn't just a movie premiere—this was an event, a cultural shift.

The Egyptian Theater, developed by entrepreneur Sid Grauman, became a destination, with ticket offices across Southern California. Agents organized bus trips from San Diego or Santa Barbara to tour Hollywood and see a movie at the Egyptian. The theater was an exemplar of the "movie palaces" being built in New York City, Chicago, Detroit, Cleveland, and other major cities. The "red-carpet premiere," also a Grauman creation, became a cultural touchstone. "It is hard to imagine the excitement that these early film shows evoked," writes economist Robert Gordon, "but many of the viewers had never traveled or had a chance to see places more than a few miles from their homes. For the first time, a person might see what a moving elephant looked like or gain a first view of a beach on the Atlantic or Pacific oceans." [2]

Behind the glamour, something larger was happening to the U.S. economy. The Egyptian Theater, with its floodlights and film projectors, was only possible thanks to one essential innovation: electricity. Without it, there would have been no lit billboards, no air-conditioned theater, no popcorn machines, and no electrically powered film reels.

This isn't just Hollywood nostalgia. It's a reminder that some technologies do more than make us faster and more efficient—they change how we *live*. Electricity didn't invent the movie entertainment industry, but it enabled it to become bigger, grander, and more accessible.

INNOVATION VS. TRANSFORMATION

Not all technologies have this power. Tractors made farming more efficient and lifted GDP, but they didn't transform daily life off the farm. Antibiotics saved lives, but their impact on GDP was subtle. Then there are the rarest of all technologies—the so-called general-purpose technologies like electricity, the internal combustion engine, and the personal computer. These don't just change work; they change how we experience the world.

This brings us to AI. Is AI more like the farm tractor—innovative for IT data scientists but incremental for others? Or is it more like the personal computer or even electricity—regime-changing and life-defining? The answer to these questions will shape the future of the U.S. economy, financial markets, and investment portfolios.

THE NEXT BIG SHIFT

In the years ahead, two powerful forces will most shape the economic outlook:

- **AI-driven transformation**: Big, bold, and full of potential *if* its J-curve advances
- **Age-driven deficits**: Slowly but steadily climbing, and quietly suffocating

This is the tug-of-war that will determine our investment future. In Chapter 4, we discussed how pivotal technology is to shifting economic growth (yes, that 97% correlation statistic). For over a century, technological breakthroughs have been the single most important factor in driving growth, not demographics. The key question facing us now is this: will AI deliver a surge in productivity even close to what electricity did 100 years ago?

The stakes are high. On one side, we have the promise of AI-fueled economic growth. On the other, we have the potential weight of fiscal deficits, aging demographics, and rising borrowing costs. Which side wins? That's not just a theoretical question. It's the most important question for anyone managing investments, building wealth for the next generation, or setting business strategy.

THE FORK IN THE ROAD

I look for the answer in two places. I first turn to the tools of my trade—data, models, and probabilities. We can use today's megatrends as signals (those blips on the radar screen from Chapter 1) to simulate millions of possible economic and financial outcomes for the Big Four:

1. Economic growth (GDP)
2. Inflation
3. Interest rates
4. Stock market returns

But data and models tell us only part of the story. As an economist, I realize that dry statistics give little sense of what daily life could be like in these scenarios. If you're 30 today, will your work be more fulfilling, more stressful, or both? If you're 65, will you feel more economically secure or financially stretched? Numbers don't adequately answer those questions. So, I will attempt to layer in human history and lived experience into this outlook. History provides us with established criteria for transformational change in society, which can help us assess AI's potential to meet these standards.

THE COMING SHIFT

This book's empirical framework helps us see further down the road. Broadly speaking, it reveals three possible futures. The twist is that the least likely is the one most economists are betting on (e.g., the consensus "status quo"). Based on megatrends' push-pull dynamics, this is where my framework says we may be headed:[3]

- **The "Status Quo" scenario (15–20% probability)**

  - *Economic and market outcomes*: The future resembles its pre-Covid past—2% real GDP growth, stable 2% inflation, and interest rates stay low—an outcome consistent with the consensus.[4]

  - *Daily life feels like*: 2017, but with video conference calls that eventually start on time.

- **The "AI Disappoints, Deficits Drag" scenario (30–40% probability)**

  - *Economic and market outcomes*: AI disappoints in its promise, failing to live up to the hype. Worker productivity remains sluggish due to a continued lack of augmentation and automation. Meanwhile, government deficits keep climbing. Higher borrowing needs from structural deficits eventually push up borrowing costs. U.S. growth becomes less exceptional and more European. Financial markets are unprepared for this outcome.

  - *Daily life feels like*: A milder remake of the 1970s, but without the disco music or oil shocks. Inflation is stubborn as deficits raise future inflation expectations. Borrowing becomes more expensive. Homeownership is out of reach for more people. By 2040, the standard living of the average worker, after inflation, has failed to meaningfully exceed that of their parents.

- **The "AI Transforms, Productivity Surges" scenario (45–55% probability)**

  - *Economic and market outcomes*: AI continues to advance at a nonlinear pace and becomes a general-purpose technology. This eventually lifts productivity more than the personal computer and the Internet by the first half of the 2030s. AI eventually sparks transformative knock-on effects, new industries, and significant job displacement. Inflation remains well in-check thanks to technology, and deficits cease to climb given higher tax revenues from stronger growth. According to my framework, the U.S. stock market in 2025 is assigning very high odds to this outcome.

- *Daily life feels like*: The 1990s, but without a dial-up modem. A surge in innovation occurs thanks to more work automation and task augmentation. A period of more progress—but also significant disruption and job displacement. Costs of living are somewhat more manageable. Standards of living for the average American household double every 30 years, not every 70.

The Risky "Status Quo" View

The main point of this chapter is simple yet profound: the status quo is a radical forecast when viewed through the lens of history. Over the past

Figure 7.1   The consensus forecast for growth in the next decade is more of the same.

Note: Figure shows the distribution of the 10-year realized average growth rate from 1920 through 2022, along with the results of the Survey of Professional Forecasters for expected real GDP growth over the next 10 years.

Source: Vanguard calculations, based on data from Davis, Brandl-Cheng, and Khang (2024)[5] and the Federal Reserve Bank of Philadelphia's First Quarter 2024 Survey of Professional Forecasters.

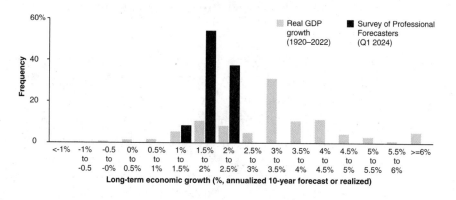

130 years, the U.S. economy has experienced significant decade-to-decade shifts, as shown in Figure 7.1. The wide dispersion in actual outcomes is evidence of shifting megatrends and their dynamic "feedback loops."

The contrast between the consensus forecast and historical patterns is stark. Between 1920 and the present, for example, megatrends have helped drive 10-year real economic growth from below 0% to above 6%. Eras filled with Skagway moments and red-carpet premieres are on the right. Eras of disappointing technology advances are on the left, including the 1970s and the "new normal" period following the 2007 Global Financial Crisis.

The consensus view seems to assume that, to the extent that megatrends matter at all, they will balance out perfectly. Now you may see why my dynamic model assigns that outcome lower odds given the tectonic plates of AI, globalization, demographics, and deficits.

THE STAKES
FOR INVESTORS

Whether you manage your own investor portfolio, direct corporate strategy, or run your own business, this chapter has two broad implications.

First, we should not plan our investments for the status quo. Megatrends move like tectonic plates, not seesaws. The consensus view is a *risky* one in its underappreciation of the elevated odds in non-consensus future outcomes.

Second, we should plan for two future paths, not one. The "AI Transforms" and "Deficits Drag" scenarios are more probable than the "status quo." We will need to evaluate portfolios that are prepared for both. The reality is that these two scenarios are not just possibilities, but probabilities. Together, the chance of one of these two non-consensus forecasts occurring is more than 75%. These probabilities will come in handy when we construct portfolios in Chapter 8.

The megatrends are telling us that there's a fork in the road up ahead. We know from Robert Frost's poem "The Road Not Taken" that the path the United States ultimately follows will make all the difference. Now let's see what each path looks like in greater detail so that we can begin to prepare ourselves and our investment portfolios.

THE "AI DISAPPOINTS, DEFICITS DRAG" SCENARIO (30–40% ODDS)

It's the year 2034, and you are preparing to drive yourself into work from your suburban home outside of Philadelphia, Pennsylvania. It's a cold January morning again, and you are growing tired of scraping frost off the car windshield. While on your commute, your favorite financial podcast is discussing the year in review for the U.S. economy and markets.

The podcaster mentions in passing what you already know and feel. Real GDP growth—that metric economists like to obsess over—has grown roughly 1% for the third straight year. The trend has weakened versus the prior decade of the 2020s. No recession or hard landing in 2033 (thankfully!), but the podcaster refers to the U. S. economy as the new Europe, and it doesn't sound like a compliment. China's GDP level has surpassed the United States for the first time. Americans have a much higher average income than those in China, but the gap continues to close.

The stock market eked out a positive return, but your equity investments haven't performed like they did a decade ago. Fixed incomes returns have been higher, though, as U.S. Treasury bonds provide a yield north of 5.5%. The podcaster compliments the Federal Reserve for keeping the rate of inflation below 3% thanks to higher interest rates on bank deposits and money market funds. But that doesn't seem to warm you as much as your car's seat warmers. Life for you and your friends is improving, and you have sleeker smartphones. Yet economic progress seems stuck in low gear. You can't shake the feeling of being a bit envious of your parent's generation, who seemed to have had it easier.

How Did This Happen?

The tug-of-war played out. *AI disappointed, and deficits won.*

Figure 7.2 summarizes the numerical outcomes from the paths the megatrends have taken. In a real sense, developments in both Silicon Valley and Washington D.C. have disappointed along the way. With the benefit of hindsight, it became apparent by 2030 that AI technologies, as a package, were not as helpful in automating and augmenting as many tasks in our work as some experts had hoped.

AI began to plateau in its ability to save time and generate new insights by the late 2020s. In this possible scenario, it turns out experts such as Robert Gordon were right in their assessment (recall Chapter 1). AI technology has not become a general-purpose technology but rather something more "incremental." In an economic sense, AI has turned out to resemble social media more than the personal computer.

AI stalled because its J-curve flattened in the late 2020s rather than continuing its upward curve of improvement and adoption like the personal computer did. As a result, only the lower bound of the time-saving estimates contemplated in Chapter 2's discussion on work's future were achieved. AI comes in at the low end of the forecast.

AI-enabled tools have led to some efficiencies in the fields of healthcare, data analytics, finance, and IT. Nevertheless, the boost has been on the order of 5–10%, not 20% or more. Nobel laureate and MIT professor Daron Acemoglu was spot-on in assessing years ago that AI's capabilities would have only minor effects on the work we do. He turned out to be correct because AI stopped improving along an S-shaped curve as it was

Figure 7.2 The dynamics and outcomes of the "AI Disappoints, Deficits Drag" scenario.

SOURCE: Author's calculations and simulations

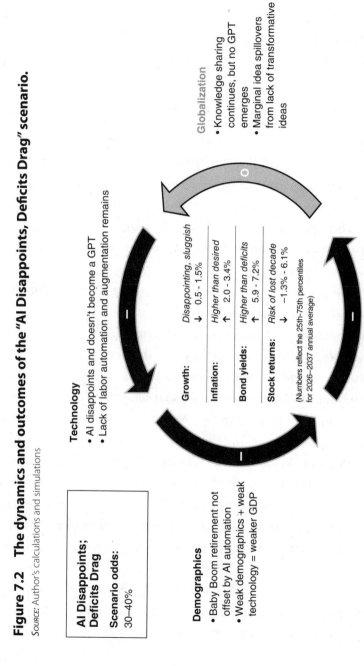

AI Disappoints; Deficits Drag

Scenario odds: 30–40%

Technology
- AI disappoints and doesn't become a GPT
- Lack of labor automation and augmentation remains

Demographics
- Baby Boom retirement not offset by AI automation
- Weak demographics + weak technology = weaker GDP

Globalization
- Knowledge sharing continues, but no GPT emerges
- Marginal idea spillovers from lack of transformative ideas

Fiscal government deficits
- Gap between spending and tax revenues widens over horizon
- Structural deficits raise inflationary expectations and bond yields, forcing higher short-term rates by the Federal Reserve

Growth:	*Disappointing, sluggish* ↘ 0.5 - 1.5%
Inflation:	*Higher than desired* ↖ 2.0 - 3.4%
Bond yields:	*Higher than deficits* ↖ 5.9 - 7.2%
Stock returns:	*Risk of lost decade* −1.3% - 6.1%

(Numbers reflect the 25th–75th percentiles for 2026–2037 annual average)

124

supposed to.[6] An unusual stalling for a computer-based technology, but it happened nonetheless.

The tasks in our jobs in 2035 are much the same as they were in 2025 because AI did not broaden its scope. AI's dystopian threat to work has turned out to be vastly overblown (again!). But greater job security has also meant some stagnation in our living standards (low rates of growth, slower advancements in pay). GenAI tools such as OpenAI's ChatGPT stalled in new capabilities by 2028, and investment in AI-related infrastructure began to slow. When you log into your personal computer at work in 2035, you are still using a keyboard, a computer mouse, and shifting through the 120 or so daily work emails you receive, just like you were in 2025.

More disappointingly, no meaningful transformative knock-on effects have occurred in fields such as healthcare or education. That's because AI has not become a general-purpose technology. There hasn't been a modern-day Skagway moment over our skies. Its absence is a tell-tale sign of more limited economic progress.

Table 7.1 attempts to paint a picture for this possible "AI Disappoints, Deficits Drag" scenario in the column along the left of the page. Most striking is the table's last row—the rate of progress in standards of living. Raj Chetty, a leading professor at Stanford University, had noted years prior that the percentage of Americans doing better financially than their parents had slowed meaningfully over time.[7]

If you're 20 or 30 or 40 years old today, that picture hasn't materially improved in the year 2035. With lower growth and more marginal ideas from technology and globalization, the status quo view has deteriorated and given way toward mild stagnation that experts such as Larry Summers worried about. Improvement occurs, but it is modest by historical standards. By 2040, some experts compare our economic performance to that of Japan.

In this very possible future, technology has failed to transform daily life as it did in the first half of the twentieth century and, to a lesser extent, in the 1990s. A Rip Van Winkle who went to sleep in 1970 and awoke in 2030 would

Table 7.1   What Our Life Could Feel Like in 2035

	"AI Disappoints, Deficits Drag" Scenario	"AI Transforms, Productivity Surges" Scenario
The commute	Human drivers still dominate the highways.	Autonomous vehicles account for majority of ridership.
The office	Work still dominated by keyboards, computer mouses, spreadsheets, and written emails.	Voice-enabled AI platforms for workers with minimal manual operations.
The world	U.S. GDP levels surpassed by China.	U.S. GDP still higher than China, and now U.S. real GDP growing at a faster rate than China.
The markets	Yields on bond funds and money market funds exceed 5%, but stock market has lagged for several years. Will take the S&P500 25 more years to double from its year-end 2024 level.	Yields on bond funds and money market funds approximately 4%. Stock market returns have cooled from the 2020s, but they outpace bond returns on average. S&P500 close to double its year-end 2024 level.
My cost of living	Costs for healthcare and education continue to exceed the average rate of inflation, making them a larger burden on the average American family.	Moderate bending in the cost curve for healthcare and education due to technological advances, helping to keep overall inflation rates low.
My health	Life expectancy little changed in 2035 at 80 years old.	Life expectancy improves by nearly 3 years, to 83 years old, in 2040 thanks to advances in medical treatments and preventive medicine, especially for those of working-age years.
My prospects	Average 30-year-old unlikely to have a better standard of living than their parents. Takes 70 years, or two generations, for the standards of living of the average American household to double.	Average 30-year-old projected to have a better standard of living than their parents. Takes 25 years, or less than one generation, for the standards of living of the average American household to double.

recognize this economic climate. He might marvel at the Internet, the smartphone, and craft beer but would have no trouble adapting to life after a 60-year nap. The shag carpeting and lime-green bathroom tile are gone, but transportation is mostly the same. Grocery stores have kiosks and smartphone apps, but otherwise are mostly the same. If Rip gets a physical, Rip must first fill out his personal information on a smart tablet (rather than a clipboard). But during the exam, the nurse or doctor will place an inflatable cuff on his forearm to take his blood pressure, just as in his 1970 physical. Afterward, he trudges off to the pharmacy to pick up some statins, a cholesterol-lowering medication introduced half a century ago.

In 1997, Nobel laureate Paul Krugman titled his book about the previous few decades of economic progress *The Age of Diminished Expectations.*[8] That phrase is an apt description of economic life in the "AI Disappoints, Deficits Drag" scenario. For most Americans, material life will be fine. Incomes will rise, albeit more slowly than they do now, and the quality of the goods and services we purchase will get a little better each year. In 2035, today's 97-inch OLED flat-screen TV[9] might be 116 inches. But you will still be staring at a TV. Change will slow, and the range of economic opportunities will narrow. Our future will be much like our present, just a little worse and with more risk of destabilizing shocks.

OUR MOST LIKELY FUTURE: AI TRANSFORMS, PRODUCTIVITY SURGES (45–55% ODDS)

It's the year 2034 back here in Philadelphia, Pennsylvania. The January weather is as cold as before, but you are no longer scraping the windshield. Your autonomous vehicle has already taken care of it, as well as its cameras, and sensors. It meets you at your front door to drive you to work. This isn't science fiction in some dystopian or utopian world. We humans still work for a living and we still do not have the Jetsons' flying cars. But the podcast's financial recap is a bit different. And personally, something feels better, too.

That's because this time in the tug-of-war, AI has won. And the U.S. economy, our jobs, and our lives have been transformed because of it. The arrows in Figure 7.3 tell us what we need to know.

Technology and globalization more than offset the potential drags from demographics and age-related deficits, thanks to more task automation and more transformative ideas in the form of new products, new treatments, and new tasks. Investment in additional electricity generation and data storage has exceeded $100 billion over the past seven years as AI usage deepens. U.S. real GDP growth averages nearly 3% between 2028 and 2035, three times the rate of the Deficits Drag scenario and close to the averages seen during the 1990s.

This productivity boom occurs because AI emerges as a general-purpose technology, transforming work in the ways detailed in Chapter 3. Nurses spend less time on record keeping and administration and more on patient care. Financial advisors spend less time recording client data and more on using AI-enabled tools to produce more customized and comprehensive advice at greater scale. Computer programmers migrate from traditional roles in writing and testing code to jobs in data science where AI-enabled insights are deeper and more impactful.

For 70% of the jobs tracked by the Department of Labor, AI-enabled automation by 2035 saves 20% of work hours, allowing us to dedicate more time to new and potentially more valuable activities. The result is a surge in productivity. GDP's path follows the J-curve, with the trend picking up by 2030. A year earlier, the future chair of the U.S. Federal Reserve makes a speech about AI that sounds similar to Chairman Greenspan's 1998 speech about the New Economy.

Figure 7.3   The dynamics and outcomes of the "AI Transforms, Productivity Surges" scenario.

Source: Author's calculations and simulations

AI Transforms
Scenario odds:
45–55%

Technology

- AI emerges as GPT, exceeding the personal computer
- Augmentation and automation accelerates, plus transformational "knock-on" effects emerge in 2030s

Globalization

- Knowledge sharing accelerates AI adoption and knock-on applications
- Ideas abroad aid in AI-related growth effects at home in U.S.

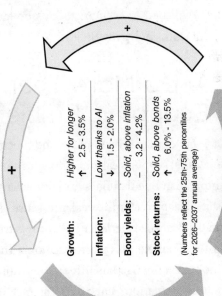

Growth:	*Higher for longer* ↑ 2.5 - 3.5%
Inflation:	*Low thanks to AI* → 1.5 - 2.0%
Bond yields:	*Solid, above inflation* – 3.2 - 4.2%
Stock returns:	*Solid, above bonds* ↑ 6.0% - 13.5%

(Numbers reflect the 25th-75th percentiles for 2026–2037 annual average)

Fiscal government deficits

- No fiscal reform, but 1990s-like growth boosts tax revenues
- Structural deficits decline in 2030s despite age-related spending

Demographics

- Baby Boom retirement partially offset by AI automation
- As in past, higher growth driven by innovation despite modestly weaker demographics
- Weaker demographics + high innovation = Higher non-inflationary GDP

Higher growth with low inflation, a sort of "Goldilocks" outcome, characterizes the early 2030s. All because the supply of new ideas, human ingenuity, and new business methods increased at a faster pace than the American population has aged. Average American living standards improve as a result. A percentage point or two of additional growth might seem modest, but compound those percentage points over 15 years. In 2024, median household income, according to the U.S. Census Bureau, totaled $80,600. If that figure rises with my GDP projections, median income in 2040 will be $127,000 in today's dollars, a 20% improvement versus a world of status quo growth.

Can AI Do More Than Enhance Economic Efficiency?

Growth of 3% is better than growth of 2% and much better than 1%. And an economic climate that supports earnings growth and equity valuations is better for us as investors than one that does not. But when I remove my green eyeshade, these statistical projections reveal little sense of the excitement, anxiety, and disruption that we will experience if AI proves transformational.

Recalling the Triangle of Transformation I introduced in the book's preface, technological change has three dimensions: augmentation, automation, and transformation. Each has distinct economic implications, with the first two relating to more labor productivity as discussed in Chapter 2. In this "AI Transforms" scenario, U.S. growth and productivity pick up beyond expectations in the coming years not simply because workers are more efficient and have more AI-enabled "power tools."

For to average 3% growth for an extended period requires that third dimension of technology—transformation—to be on par with that of the personal computer a generation ago. The power of this book's framework is the quantification of the odds and magnitudes of these potential impacts. But my framework is silent on where such transformative effects could occur. For that, we'll have to look elsewhere.

In Which Field Will the Transformation Occur?

For AI and other technologies to become transformative, AI will need to enable *new* services and applications that have their own positive knock-on effects to either growth or well-being. These are several promising technologies in the marketplace and labs today:

- Autonomous transportation[10]
- AI-powered exoskeletons for physical-trades workers[11]
- Quantum computing
- Grid-level battery storage (to store, say, solar energy and help meet AI's demand)[12]
- Advanced medical treatments (including genetic sequencing and GLP-1 receptors)[13]

Each area shows some promise in boosting productivity and output in coming years, although some would boost growth more than others. One can assess that, loosely, based upon several criteria, including (1) AI's current abilities, (2) the other complementary technologies needed to see advancement and the timeline of actual widespread commercial deployment, (3) whether the new technology simply replaces an existing technology, and (4) and the size of the unmet needs that exist from the vantage point of most Americans.

A *Potential* Area of Transformation

Against these criteria, AI-based transformation could have its greatest impact on **healthcare**, specifically improved outcomes that enhance worker health and, hence, longevity. Let me be clear: I am *not* speculating that this will happen; rather, I am identifying an area that in my judgment where it would *need* to happen for technology to have had a broader transformational effect on society.

Why healthcare? For one, healthcare plays a critical role in working-age health, longevity, and quality of life. Currently, there are roughly 12 million 25–64-year-olds who cannot work due to a disability, equating to about 7% of the entire labor force. That is a large number. An additional 4 million workers reported that a disability/illness limited them from working in their desired occupation or preferred number of hours.[14]

We'll never get these numbers to zero, but some medical experts believe that AI-powered advancements could make a dent. In 2022, there were 832,000 deaths among those under age 65, equating to 25.6 million years of potential life lost.[15] Since 1999, the death rate has risen for 20–60-year-olds while declining for all other age groups, in no small part due to the opioid crisis. Table 7.2 lists the top 10 causes of premature death in the United States.

Table 7.2   Leading Causes of Death in the United States for Working-Age Population, 2022

Cause	Years of Potential Life Lost
Malignant Neoplasms	4,014,431
Heart Disease	3,476,770
Unintentional Poisoning (overdoses)	3,196,012
Suicide	1,396,507
Motor Vehicle Accidents	1,352,011
COVID-19	1,073,234
Homicide	1,005,333
Liver Disease	838,203
Perinatal Mortality	762,976
Diabetes	762,976

Source: CDC National Center for Health Statistics, National Vital Statistics System

Technological advances in the years ahead *could* reduce some of this lost life. Automobile accidents, for instance, could experience a substantial reduction via new AI-safety features (blind-spot detection, collision warnings) and fully autonomous driving. Others like heart disease, liver disease, diabetes, and overdose deaths may see improvement from a suite of pharmaceuticals such of GLP-1 drugs that lower obesity and reduce alcohol and drug dependencies.

Something Similar Has Happened Before

Whether such improvement occurs remains to be seen. If the unfortunate statistics in Table 7.2 saw a reduction of 10–20% over the next 10 years, that would be sufficient to modestly improve overall longevity numbers, well-being, and even labor force participation rates.

Past technologies have had similar positive effects in unexpected ways. About a decade before the night of Hollywood's first red-carpet movie premiere, millions of Americans were working in manufacturing plants. Prior to electrification, employment in manufacturing was a brutal, dirty, and dangerous affair. Industrial fatalities in the early 1900s were estimated at 61 deaths per 100,000 workers, some 15 times higher than today's rate. Documented in Crystal Eastman's *Work Accidents and the Law* (1910), tragedies like the following near Pittsburgh, Pennsylvania were all too common across the country:

- "William Rock, fourteen years old, employed by the Pittsburgh Brewing Company at Duquesne, on November 14, 1906, while trying to put a belt on a pulley, was caught up in the machinery and killed."
- "Clifford Rea, a boy of eighteen, was oiling machinery for the Union Storage Company. In order to oil one machine, he had to go into a space thirteen inches wide, between a heavy sliding door and a

revolving flywheel. While he was there the door was suddenly opened; Rea instinctively leaned back a little and was instantly caught in the wheel."

But with electrification, things slowly improved. Manufacturing facilities transitioned away from the steam-powered drives and pulleys that were often the cause of workplace fatalities. These electricity-powered facilities improved air quality and workers' visual perception via electric lightning. In future decades, the rise of labor unions and regulatory agencies like Occupational Safety and Health Administration (OSHA) would make even greater contributions to safer work practices. But electricity played a surprisingly positive role.

Here's to hoping that technology positively surprises us again.

HEADWINDS + TAILWINDS = TWO SCENARIOS

The odds are approximately 45–55% that AI will become a transformative technology, boosting economic growth and transforming the way we live and work. But my analytical framework reveals that this optimistic projection will be challenged by the nontrivial probability that AI fails to deliver its expected benefits. Rising deficits, driven by demographic change, could overtake the megatrend of technology if AI's J-curve is weaker than some hope. That combination would hinder U.S. economic growth—a future worse than our present. I wish that the odds of this outcome were lower, but they're not. The odds are 30–40%. This is why the tug-of-war between these two outcomes will be the most consequential economic battle over the next 15 years. Odds are less than 20% for anything in-between.

The stakes are high—for workers, investors, and policymakers. But this tug-of-war is nothing new. Megatrends have always competed. In "An

Essay on the Principle of Population" (1798), Thomas Malthus argued that population growth would lead to war, famine, and disease. In 1798, the world's population totaled 800 million. But in 2022, eight billion humans inhabited a richer society. Technological progress neutralized the Malthusian warning that "the power of population is indefinitely greater than the power in the earth to produce subsistence for man."

In the coming tug-of-war, my simulations suggest that—more likely than not—technology will help us prevail. We will innovate faster than we age. The odds are favorable, but the outcome is far from certain. The verdict is not yet in because the battle has just begun.

As investors, it is critical that we plan for two future paths, not one. The "AI Transforms" and "Deficit Drag" scenarios are more probable than the "status quo." We will need to evaluate portfolios that are prepared for both. We can do this by following the lead of Vanguard founder Jack Bogle. He advocated the power of balance, costs, and diversification as we investors gaze up at the skies taking the long view.

In the following chapter, I provide more context for this timeless investment philosophy, one that will help us adapt to whatever economic climate develops.

NOTES

1. As reported in https://www.hollywoodreporter.com/movies/movie-news/robin-hood-1922-movie-premiere-1235242865/.
2. Gordon, R. J. (2016). *The Rise and Fall of American growth*. Princeton University Press.
3. Based on the simulations, one can calculate specific probabilities for these three scenarios, which include "deeper tails" that are even better or worse (e.g., a future depression) economic outcomes than what I verbally describe. However, those scenarios account for less than 6% of all simulations. To reduce the appearance of over-precision, I have rounded the three scenario probabilities into ranges. For full disclosure, the estimated probabilities for average

annualized real GDP growth over the 2026–2037 period in each of the three scenarios are as follows: (1) "Status Quo" scenario—17.0%; (2) "AI Disappoints, Deficits Drag" scenario—34.5%; (3) "AI Transforms, Productivity Surges" scenario—48.5%.

4. When I say "consensus view," I refer to projections of leading institutions such as the Federal Reserve Board, the Congressional Budget Office, and the Federal Reserve Bank of Philadelphia's "Survey of Professional Forecasters." The Federal Reserve doesn't specify a time frame for "longer-run projections," noting only that it represents the Federal Open Market Committee members' "assessment of the value to which each variable would be expected to converge, over time, under appropriate monetary policy and in the absence of further shocks to the economy. The Federal Reserve Bank of Philadelphia's Survey of Professional Forecasters (SPF) can be found at https://www.philadelphiafed.org.

5. Davis, J. H., and Lukas, B. C. (2024). "Megatrends and the U.S. Economy, 1890–2040." Social Science Research Network, 1 Jan. 2024," https://doi.org/10.2139/ssrn.4702028.

6. Acemoglu, D., "The Simple Macroeconomics of AI," MIT working paper, 2024, at https://economics.mit.edu/sites/default/files/2024-04/The%20Simple%20Macroeconomics%20of%20AI.pdf.

7. Raj Chetty, et al. *The Fading American Dream: Trends in Absolute Income Mobility since 1940.* NBER Working Paper 22910. December, 2016. https://www.nber.org/system/files/working_papers/w22910/w22910.pdf.

8. https://mitpress.mit.edu/9780262611343/the-age-of-diminished-expectations/.

9. https://www.lg.com/us/tvs/lg-oled97g2pua-oled-tv.

10. For more reading on autonomous driving systems, see McGillis (2023). https://manhattan.institute/article/why-we-need-self-driving-technology-and-how-we-can-get-it-faster.

11. For more reading on intelligent exoskeletons, see Lee (2024). https://www.nature.com/articles/s41528-024-00297-0.

12. See "Greening the Grid" (2019). https://www.nrel.gov/docs/fy19osti/74426.pdf.

13. See Zheng (2024). https://www.nature.com/articles/s41392-024-01931-z.

14. BLS Current Population Survey (October 2024).

15. Years of potential life lost is a measure of premature mortality, calculated by subtracting the age of death from age 75.

CHAPTER EIGHT

PREPARING FOR THE TUG-OF-WAR: PRINCIPLES vs. DOGMA

JACK BOGLE'S MENTOR

After graduating from Princeton University in 1920, Walter L. Morgan joined a Philadelphia accounting firm to produce financial statements for local businesses. He qualified as Pennsylvania's youngest Certified Public Accountant. He earned $28 a week. "When I asked for a raise, my boss told me he wasn't particularly smitten with my work," Morgan recalled in a 1998 interview.[1]

"I promptly left for another firm, which assigned me to help individuals prepare their tax returns. I helped quite a number of people—and people with money—and it didn't take me long to realize that they needed investment counsel as well as tax advice. I gathered some money from business associates and family members and pooled it into a single fund to buy stocks and bonds." That fund, launched in 1929, is Vanguard Wellington Fund, the nation's first balanced mutual fund. Today, the fund actively manages more than $110 billion on behalf of clients saving for education, retirement, and other long-term goals.[2]

The fund's longevity is a testament to investment principles that have helped it navigate almost 100 years of changing economic and financial conditions. When Morgan launched the Wellington Fund,[3] "There were a number of closed-end funds that invested predominantly in stocks using borrowed money to get high leverage," he said. "With such funds selling at tremendous premiums—as high as 260 times asset value[4]—and regular stocks selling at 60 times earnings, I figured that people were going to get sorry results if they bought either of them."

He was right. From 1929 to 1939, the U.S. stock market produced a negative return. "I thought it would be better to have a balanced fund that held common and preferred stocks as well as high-quality corporate and government bonds," Morgan said. "By holding fixed-income instruments, you reduced your risk in the event the stock market went down." During the 1930s, Wellington Fund returned a cumulative 10%, a modest but notable gain during one of the worst decades in U.S. financial market history.

Like Benjamin Graham in his 1949 investment classic *The Intelligent Investor*, Morgan emphasized the importance of diversification across stocks and bonds. At the time, diversification through individual security selection was impossible for all but the wealthiest investors. In the early 1950s, according to the Brookings Institution, the small number of Americans who participated in the stock market held a median of just two stocks.[5] With a mutual fund, Morgan explained, "Professional investment advice and diversification could be had at a reasonable cost."

FOUR INVESTMENT PRINCIPLES

In 1951, recent college graduate Jack Bogle joined his fellow Princeton alumnus at Wellington Management's offices at 1420 Walnut Street in Philadelphia. As a college senior, Bogle had interviewed Walter Morgan for his thesis, "The Economic Role of the Investment Company."[6] Bogle sent a copy of his thesis to Walter Morgan, who offered him a job. Bogle accepted. Morgan announced Bogle's hiring in a memo to his associates: "A pretty good piece of work for a fellow in college without any practical experience in business life. Largely as a result of this thesis, we have added Mr. Bogle to our Wellington organization."[7]

Bogle internalized Morgan's belief in the importance of balance and diversification. Over the next 68 years, Bogle, a great communicator and

Figure 8.1   Jack Bogle drafts a speech.
Note the photo of Jack Bogle and Walter L. Morgan over Bogle's right shoulder.
Source: Vanguard History Center

educator, translated these beliefs into lessons to guide a successful investment program (see Figure 8.1). The serendipitous pairing of these investment pioneers produced principles that can help us succeed in any investment environment. The investment tools at our disposal have grown since then, but the principles we rely upon to execute our investment plan remain timeless.

CORE PRINCIPLES

Bogle articulated these principles in hundreds of speeches, countless articles, and 12 books, an intellectual foundation that his successors and my research team have tried to build on. This investment philosophy—shared by other investment legends from Benjamin Graham to Burt Malkiel to Warren Buffett—can be distilled into four principles:[8]

1. **Goals**: Create clear, realistic investment goals for your portfolio, incorporating your time horizon and an honest assessment of your tolerance for risk. Central to this principle is the power of saving. The value an investor's portfolio achieves over time is the sum of their savings (either in one lump-sum or in regular contributions over time) and their investment returns.

   Time plays a critical role in determining the savings needed to achieve an investment goal. Even over long horizons, the importance of the savings rate (which we can control) can rival or even exceed that of returns from the financial markets (which we cannot). Assume a 4% net-of-inflation investment return and equal annual contributions over a 30-year time horizon. In this hypothetical example, investment returns and savings contribute roughly the same dollar amount to one's investment goal.[9] Over the first 10 years in this example, however, savings contribute 80% of the total, dwarfing the relative importance of market returns.

2. **Balance**: Maintain a diversified mix of broad investments. Diversification across different kinds of investments reduces a portfolio's exposure to the risk common to an entire asset class such as stocks and bonds. My portfolio construction model demonstrates that exposure to some bonds can enhance the risk-adjusted returns of the most aggressive, stock-heavy portfolios. And conservative bond-heavy strategies can benefit from some stock exposure. Other asset classes, including alternative investments, can have a role under certain conditions.

   Diversification within an asset class reduces your exposure to risks associated with a given company or sector. It has mitigated the risk of disaster when, say, technology stocks collapsed in the early 2000s or big banks and brokerages flirted with or succumbed to bankruptcy during the Global Financial Crisis. As Morgan explained, one of the great benefits of mutual (and today exchange-traded) funds is diversification for investors without the wealth, expertise, or interest to build their own portfolios of individual securities. In 2019, my colleagues estimated that the historical shift from individual stocks to mutual and exchange-traded funds (ETFs) had produced a cumulative investor welfare benefit—a calculation that accounts for return, risk, and investor preferences—of $730 billion.[10] That benefit is no doubt multiples higher today.

   As I explore portfolios for the next decade, some portfolios may favor particular market segments—"value stocks" in a broad ETF or mutual fund with above-market earnings yields or corporate bond ETFs that yield more than government bonds. But all portfolios are diversified. There's no risk that an outsized position in a modern Enron or Lehman Brothers will destroy the portfolio's performance.

3. **Minimize cost and fees**: This was perhaps Bogle's greatest contribution to investors and the financial services industry. As Bogle

often said, "In investing, you get what you don't pay for." Assume an annual return of 6%. With annual costs equal to 0.1% of assets, a $100,000 investment will grow to $557,383 after 30 years. If annual costs are 2.0%, the total will be just $317,081, some $240,000 less. When higher costs compound, the differences in your wealth can be staggering.

Costs—which include taxes and investment costs such as expense ratios, transaction costs, and sales charges—have a clear bearing on net-of-cost returns. While several factors (market and otherwise) determine fund performance, the inverse relationship between costs and net-of-cost returns is a strong one in investments. When you examine more than 8,000 equity mutual funds in the 10 years through 2022, for example, the lowest-cost fund quartile (the 25% of funds with an average expense ratio of 0.57%) averaged an annualized net-of-cost return of 8.7%. The same average return from the highest-cost fund quartile (the 25% of funds with an average expense ratio of 2.47%) was only 5.7%.

Bogle produced volumes of research about the "tyranny of compounding costs," the enemy of the "magic of compounding returns." I also like *Wall Street Journal* columnist Jason Zweig's phrase about the danger of high costs: the "black magic of de-compounding."[11] My strategies for the next decade can be implemented with low-cost stock and bond funds and ETFs. Whatever returns the financial markets provide, the investor will reap just about all of them.

4. **Discipline**: Discipline, the ability to stick with a research-based investment plan through good times and bad, is the most important principle and the most challenging to uphold. Investing evokes strong emotions that can lead to impulsive decisions—panic selling during market volatility or return-chasing during market booms.

These four principles share an overarching theme: Focus on the things that you can control—costs, investment horizon, and risk. They are not intended to prescribe a one-size-fits-all portfolio; they are instead core tenets that should underlie the different portfolio approaches. Today, I believe every investment professional and financial advisor would agree with them. That is a powerful legacy.

DEBUNKING DOGMA

As the global head of Vanguard's Investment Strategy Group, I have the pleasure of leading one of the largest research teams in the asset-management industry. Former Vanguard CEO Jack Brennan founded our research team nearly 22 years ago to build on Bogle's work in developing prudent asset allocation strategies and perspectives for a range of clients and goals. We have produced hundreds of reports and analytical tools since then and collaborated with other leading thinkers on a range of important topics. My group's research contributes directly to the methodologies and guidelines for multi-asset portfolios relied upon by all types of investors, from advisor ETF model portfolios to 401(k) plan target date funds.

One of my team's jobs, oddly enough, is to address interpretations of these investment principles that can risk reducing them to unproductive dogma. The principle to "minimize cost," for example, might be overinterpreted as "thou shalt not buy actively managed funds." After all, low-cost actively managed funds have higher costs than their index fund counterparts.

But dogma fails to reflect nuance in my team's research that informs these principles. Worse, it can limit an investor's flexibility to act on the spirit and letter of these principles as economic and market environments change. I address three pieces of dogma to set the stage for discussion about portfolios designed for the tug-of-war between competing megatrends over the next 10–15 years. I address these dogmas with reference to a target client whose objectives are consistent with a 60/40 stock/bond strategic allocation; this hypothetical investor is also willing to take on some active risk in the pursuit of modestly higher returns.

The first dogma: "Active strategies have no role in a portfolio."

The research reality: Most actively managed funds fail to outperform their passively managed counterparts. Long-term success in active strategies, whether in private or public markets, requires both skilled managers and accessing them at a modest cost.

Let me be crystal clear: the *average* active manager has absolutely no role in anyone's portfolio. Why? Because in any market (whether it's efficient or not), 50% of the actively traded dollars will outperform the other 50% of dollars, before costs. After costs, then, the average dollar underperforms the market. Professor Burton Malkiel of Princeton University, author of one of the greatest investment books ever written in *A Random Walk Down Wall Street* (1973, 2023 12th edition), denounces the performance of the average active stock fund in the introduction of that book's 50th anniversary edition. He writes:

> An investor with $10,000 to invest at the start of 1977 … would have a portfolio worth $2,143,500 at the start of 2022, assuming all dividends were reinvested. A second investor who instead purchased shares in the average actively managed mutual fund would have seen the investment grow to $1,477,033. The difference is astonishing. Through January 1, 2022, the index investor was ahead by $666,467, or a staggering two-thirds of a million dollars. (pp.19–20).

Of course, *some* active managers do, in fact, meet the dual criteria that are necessary for enduring success in active strategies: managers that possess both considerable skill and offering that skill to clients at low costs. Although Bogle popularized index-fund investing, I consider his most important legacy his emphasis on low costs.

In an interview with Morningstar's Christine Benz and Jeff Ptak, Bloomberg analyst Eric Balchunas, author of *The Bogle Effect*, says, "I think index funds get way too much credit for the index fund revolution; I really do. If they weren't cheap, they just would not be sweeping the nation the way they are, and eventually, probably the world. But low cost is really everything."[12]

Data shows that active managers with lower fees and active skill can outperform the market, although it requires patience on the part of the investor. My team's research has found that outperforming managers frequently endure prolonged periods of underperformance.[13] For example, an active equity fund or ETF may lag the market for several years before delivering outsized or "lumpy" gains. With patience, skilled managers who can identify mispriced securities in a fairly efficient market at a reasonable price can deliver positive excess returns over the market.

The second dogma: "The venerable U.S. policy portfolio—60% U.S. stocks, 40% U.S. bonds—implemented with market cap weighted index funds is the only viable strategy."

The research reality: Broader diversification across asset classes and market segments can enhance your chances of long-term success.

The all-indexed, market cap 60/40 portfolio is an exceptionally sound investment portfolio whose strong track record serves as the canonical benchmark for many investors. It is also a portfolio that many active strategies fail to beat. While this portfolio can serve an excellent starting point,[14] it is not the only viable strategy. Deviations from broad market cap exposure to overweight certain global stock or bond market segments can be completely appropriate for investors based on their income needs, risk preferences, or a forward-looking view of risks and returns. This logic certainly extends to non-U.S. stock and bond allocations, but it can also extend to private investments. Private equity investments, for instance, can have a role for certain clients if (and I would stress, only if) one appropriately takes into account their illiquidity, the criticality in identifying top-performing active managers, and the ability to access those managers at a reasonable cost.[15] The point is that while investors can view the 60/40 U.S. portfolio as a solid reference benchmark, they need not interpret it as inviolable dogma.

The third dogma: "'Staying the course' means never changing your asset allocation."

The research reality: We can capitalize on long-term signals to make measured changes in our asset allocations as the economic and financial climate changes.

Since incorporating The Vanguard Group, Bogle championed long-term investing with a simple yet powerful principle: "Stay the course." This philosophy emphasizes maintaining a well-diversified, low-cost portfolio consistent with one's risk tolerance and financial goals. Bogle also recognized that portfolio risks shift as megatrends shift and technology sparks profound (some would say *irrational*) excitement. The dot-com bubble of the late 1990s was the most pronounced period of speculation and exuberance in the past 150 years. During that period, stock market valuations exceeded those before the 1929 stock market crash. In his research, Bogle explored strategies to make measured changes in a portfolio allocation based on the relative values of stocks, bonds, and different market sectors. These measured changes were intended as a measure of risk management, not a blind pursuit of "tactical outperformance."

In the next chapter, I assess the relative values, and expected returns, among asset classes and market sectors. These probability-weighted assessments are the basis for my risk-mitigating departures from a long-term strategic portfolio, again for investors with at least a moderate risk tolerance. In my view, investors can consider modest asset allocation changes within a systematic process not as an attempt to be smarter than the market but as an effort to be more prudent in circumstances of radical change in the relative valuation of different asset classes and market segments.[16]

Consider this simple example. If an investor needs to draw 4% a year from their portfolio for their spending needs, should they maintain the same stock-bond mix when high-quality bond yields are at 7%

as when they are at 2%? Again, any change in one's asset allocation should be in moderation and undertaken to narrow the range of future long-run outcomes. As interest rates touched historical lows and interest income vanished from 2010 to 2020, one could have made a case for a slightly higher strategic allocation to stocks, with their potential to boost dividend income over time. (As discussed previously, however, a return to the era of sound money[17] means microscopic interest rates are no longer a problem.)

CONCLUSION: MEGATRENDS AND OUR PORTFOLIO

Four investment principles—clear goals, diversification, low costs, and discipline—are as relevant today as ever. These tenets can help us navigate market uncertainty, avoid emotional mistakes, and harness the compounding portfolio effects of market returns. But as I have noted, the impulse to reduce these principles to dogma can limit our ability to prepare our portfolios for a different future.

Actively managed funds can play a beneficial role in a portfolio when one identifies skilled, low-cost managers and one has the patience to endure their inevitable periods of underperformance. Broad market cap portfolios are a robust starting point but are not the only option, even if they are the benchmark that other strategies should be judged against. And while "staying the course" is critical, it doesn't mean ignoring risks on the horizon. Indeed, it can involve making valuation-aware changes in your portfolio to protect against growing downside risks.

With these principles in hand and dogma addressed, we have a framework for navigating the coming tug-of-war of competing megatrends. As technology, demographics, globalization, and debt reshape the financial landscape, we can rely on these investment principles. Change is coming, but we have a plan. Now I'll share a stay-the-course strategy that addresses the tug-of-war risk that we will face.

One of the greatest naval battles ever waged provides a plan of attack.

NOTES

1. itv_199807 | Vanguard Digital Archive. Note: Interview with John Woerth.
2. Author's Note: This is the only time I will mention a specific fund or investment product of my employer. I do so here only because I believe it is fundamental to the story. The Vanguard Wellington Fund is administered by Vanguard but managed by Wellington Management Company.
3. The fund was originally named the Industrial Power and Securities Company to call forth imagery of a vigorous American industry but was renamed in 1935.
4. Today, closed-end funds are obscure participants in the investment management industry, supplanted by mutual funds and exchange-traded funds (ETFs). Closed-end funds sometimes trade at a premium, sometimes at a discount, to the value of their holdings.
5. Kimmel, L. (1952). *Share Ownership in the United States*. Washington, D.C.: Brookings Institution.
6. In the regulatory language, a mutual fund is referred to as an "Investment Company."
7. Bogle, J. C. (2010). *Common Sense on Mutual Funds*. Hoboken, N.J.: Wiley. Page 536.
8. Some of my discussion here is drawn from the publication *Vanguard's Principles for Investing Success* (2023). One can find additional details in that publication at https://corporate.vanguard.com/content/dam/corp/research/pdf/vanguards_principles_for_investing_success.pdf.
9. See Vanguard (2023, ibid; p. 6).
10. https://www.pm-research.com/content/iijindinv/11/1/6.
11. https://jasonzweig.com/the-long-sordid-history-of-high-fees-for-low-returns.
12. https://www.morningstar.com/funds/eric-balchunas-assessing-jack-bogles-monumental-legacy#transcript.

13. See, for instance, two companion Vanguard white papers published in 2024 on this topic: Considerations for active fund investing and Considerations for index fund investing.

14. I should add "or similar all-indexed, market cap portfolios with a different asset allocation based on an investor's goals." That could span the entire spectrum of possibilities in a stock-bond portfolio, from an aggressive 100/0 stock/bond allocation to a conservative 0/100 stock/bond allocation.

15. These last two caveats for private investments are identical to those I stressed for active funds, as long-term success in either possess the same requirements. Whether or not someone may label private equity or another alternative investment an "asset class" (implying you should have an allocation) is, in my opinion, irrelevant since there is not an investable index for such private investments. Unfortunately, I have seen too many investment committees make the mistake of allocating to private investments (say, 20% of their portfolio) on the grounds of diversification, only to underperform due to poor manager or strategy selection. Any allocation to private investments involves active risk since it cannot be implemented using index funds that hold the entire private market. If my talent and cost requirements are met, my team's research shows the performance of your overall portfolio can improve, sometimes dramatically.

16. The critical distinction between market timing and risk control is stressed on page 246 in Jack's book, *Bogle on Mutual Funds* (1993, republished 2015, Wiley). In that book, Jack believed that certain investors could allow the stock-bond weight of their portfolio change as much as perhaps 15% (and no more) based on such expected return ranges. This approach is consistent with the modern concept of time-varying asset allocation (TVAA). TVAA permits modest, systematic shifts in stock-bond or related allocations based on valuation signals, macroeconomic shifts, and return expectations. This approach doesn't involve trying to "time the market" but rather follows a gradual, disciplined process for rebalancing a portfolio based on long-term fundamentals while accounting for inherent market uncertainty. Nevertheless, this is an active strategy because it deviates from a client's strategic allocation and risks underperformance even if intended to control for risk. For more details on my team's research, please see "Our time-varying portfolio and a dynamic economy."

17. Davis, J. "Savers Will Benefit From a Return to Sound Money". Op-Ed in *The Wall Street Journal,* January 30, 2023. wsj.com/articles/a-return-to-sound-moneywill-be-a-boon-for-savers-bond-savings-interestyield-stability-vanguard-inflation-fed-11675107380?msockid=24937982b07360e22ce96cbab1c3617a.

CHAPTER NINE

A VICTOR'S PORTFOLIO, ACT I: DIVIDE AND CONQUER

THE BATTLE OF THE NILE

On August 1, 1798, *Zealous* and *Goliath*—British warships that had pursued Napoleon and the French Navy through the Mediterranean Sea since April—found the French fleet anchored in Aboukir Bay near Egypt's Nile Delta. The captains signaled their commander, Rear Admiral Horatio Nelson, who was 9 miles away on the HMS *Vanguard*. Nelson directed his fleet to Aboukir Bay.

The French had anchored their fleet close to shore. Following convention, the French fleet was filed in a long battle line, with the ships' port (left) sides facing the shore. This map in Figure 9.1, drawn years later, shows the single-filed French fleet in dark dots. French Admiral François-Paul Brueys ordered this conventional position because he reasoned that the shallow, rocky waters between the ships and shore would protect his fleet from attack on that port (left) side. The starboard (or right) sides faced seaward, with guns and cannon trained on what seemed to be the only approach for any combatant.

Figure 9.1   The British and French Navies meet in the Battle of the Nile, 1798.

Source: From Plan of the Battle of the Nile, 1798. Illustration by Westall. From the book *The Life of Nelson* by Robert Southey published London, 1883. (Photo by Universal History Archive/Getty Images).

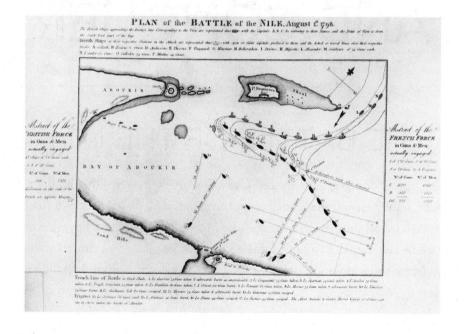

THE FRENCH FLEET COMES INTO VIEW

By 4 p.m. that day, Nelson's armada entered the bay, 3 miles from the French fleet. As the French fleet came into view, Lord Nelson trained his eyeglass on their position in the bay and devised his strategy. At 5:30 p.m., Admiral Nelson ordered his captains to "form a battle line as most convenient," giving his captains some discretion to maneuver in facing the larger enemy fleet.[1] *Goliath* sailed ahead into the shallow waters between the French fleet and the shore—a risky decision given the bay's reefs and shoals but a path the French were not expecting. More notably, *Lord Nelson and his captains were breaking with consensus in splitting their fleet.* But it was part of the plan. To take two paths, not one. According to George Elliot, a *Goliath* midshipman, Captain Thomas Foley said that "he should not be surprised to find the Frenchman unprepared for action on the inner side."[2]

TWO PATHS, NOT ONE

Foley was right. The French ships were undefended on their port sides, positioned for only one side in this coming battle. "On some of their ships, the larboard gun ports were blocked by spare equipment and other gear that had been hastily piled on the shoreward side as the English approached."[3] Four British ships followed the *Goliath*, firing on the French ships' undefended flank. Admiral Nelson led the rest of his fleet to attack the French on their starboard side. Now the British cannons were pummeling the French fleet from both sides in a crossfire.

The French fleet was caught in the middle in this tug-of-war. At 10 p.m., the *Orient*, the pride of the French navy, exploded, killing Admiral Brueys as flames reached the gunpowder stored below deck. Although much of the French fleet had surrendered, the fighting continued through August 2. On the morning of August 3, Admiral Nelson sent two ships to force the surrender of the remaining French fleet. Two French ships escaped, but the battle was over. "The strategic impact of the battle was dramatic," writes historian Roger Knight. "At a stroke it restored Britain's supremacy in the Mediterranean, which it held for the rest of the wars against France."[4]

TWO NAUTICAL LESSONS

I relay this magnificent story not for its nautical history. Yes, it is true I work at Vanguard, a firm that Jack Bogle named after Admiral Nelson's flagship. In fact, I work in the Goliath building, namesake of the warship that led the attack on the French fleet's undefended portside. Every day, I pass by a reproduction of that same Battle of the Nile map hanging in the Goliath lobby.

But what is more important about this more than 200-year-old battle are the two lessons I believe it can teach us about the economy and about investing.

A NAUTICAL LESSON FOR ECONOMISTS

The first lesson is meant for me, as an economist. As illustrated again in Figure 9.2, the British and French fleets took different paths—three paths in fact: an expected middle one by the French and two unexpected paths by the British. In economic terms, the French fleet followed the narrow-and-straight consensus path, and it was well reasoned. It assumed the status quo of typical naval battles would unfold.

Figure 9.2   We can prepare for our economic future with lessons from the Battle of the Nile.

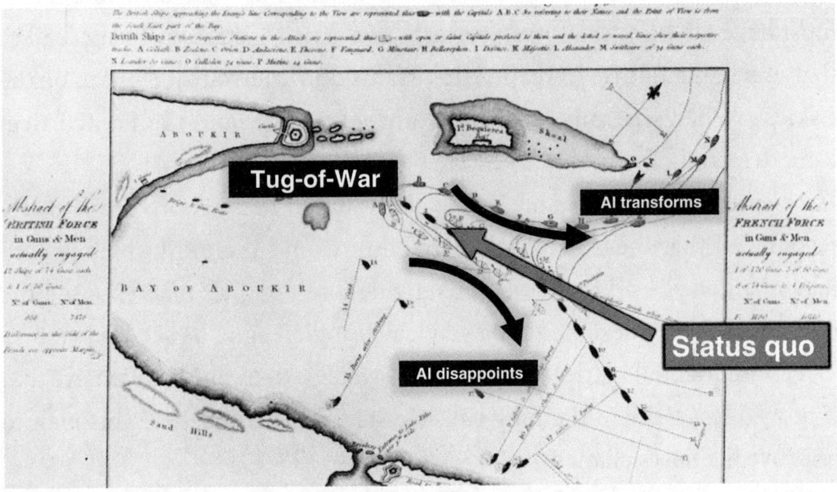

Lord Nelson, on the other hand, divided his fleet. The ships of the Royal British Navy each took one of two different paths. This response was unexpected by the French, a personal reminder that the "status quo" view of the world did not prevail. Visually and figuratively to me, the tug-of-war paths taken by the British fleet symbolize the likely—and as of yet, undetermined—paths the U.S. economy will take in the years ahead. But, as was *not* the case for the Royal Navy, the path that the economy takes will be either one or the other. It will not be both.

A NAUTICAL LESSON FOR INVESTORS

The lesson for investing comes from the ship captains. The strategies adopted by French Admiral Brueys and British Admiral Nelson illustrate different approaches to planning for the future and managing risk. Brueys thought that the future could follow only one path. And, to be fair, it must have seemed like it was the most probable path—so probable that it must have felt like certainty. He executed a sensible strategy to succeed in that inevitable future. In reality, the "status quo" view turned out to be the riskiest. When that future failed to unfold, Brueys and the French fleet were defeated.

Nelson, on the other hand, saw the value in being more prudent. He recognized that there is no inevitable future, and the most obvious path may not always lead to victory. His divide-and-conquer plan exposed the risks of a strategy designed for a single possibility—and he secured victory in a consequential battle. Lord Nelson's strategy went on the offensive, but it proved less risky in the long run. He stayed the course with his plan to improve his fleet's chances.

To any investor who's looking to build a portfolio for the next decade or more, the contrast between Brueys and Nelson imparts important investment lessons, such as weighting probabilities of different scenarios like authors Nate Silver and Annie Duke describe. Let me share why both approaches are so relevant in today's return environment as we look to build portfolios for the coming decade.

THE RESILIENCE OF BALANCED PORTFOLIOS

Well-diversified stock-bond portfolios, such as the 60/40, have become a well-prescribed investment strategy and benchmark for good reason. For more than a century, a 60/40 U.S.-only strategy has delivered—on average—approximately 8% annualized nominal returns (see Figure 9.3). An 8% average annual return is an impressive track record that would be the envy

Figure 9.3   Since 1900, the 60/40 portfolio has delivered an impressive average return.

The chart shows the average annualized return by decade after adjusting for inflation (top) and in nominal returns (bottom).

SOURCE: Author's calculations based on the S&P500 Index from Robert Shiller's website and returns on a 10-year constant maturity bond yield. These returns would differ somewhat from even broader portfolios such as an all-capitalization U.S. stock market index and U.S. bond market index, whose data are only available for more recent periods

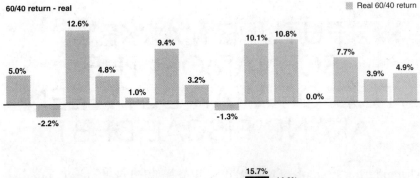

of many investments. When one nets out the effects of inflation, the "real" or inflation-adjusted returns have averaged roughly 4% per year. Such robust returns have enabled investors to meet their long-term goals such as spending in retirement, funding institutional or university needs, and bequeathing wealth to future generations.

However, balanced portfolios have not always had smooth sailing. Certain decades, such as the 1940s, the 1970s, and the 2000s, brought more disappointing returns. In other decades, the average returns have exceeded a stellar 10% per year. These decade-by-decade fluctuations often correspond to shifting megatrends, a recurring theme throughout this book. The rise in fiscal deficits and lack of technological change played a role in the negative real returns of the 1970s. The boom times of the Roaring 1920s and New Economy 1990s boosted portfolio returns well in excess of their long-run averages, with future returns sometimes experiencing a "hard landing" as valuations came back down to Earth.

FUTURE MARKET SCENARIOS: THE TUG-OF-WAR BETWEEN AI AND FISCAL DEBT

The enduring strength of balanced, well-diversified portfolios lies in their ability to diversify risk, smoothing volatility across various economic conditions. But there are macroeconomic regimes where balanced portfolios do better than others. The rest of this chapter explores how megatrends such as AI and rising fiscal debt might shape the performance of stocks, bonds, and balanced portfolios over the next decade.

A benefit of this book's framework is that it can translate the paths of megatrends and other factors (ranging from Federal Reserve policy to commodity-price shocks) with the returns on stocks, bonds, and other investments. For every simulated path that the U.S. economy may take, there is an associated path for bond and stock returns and the diversification each may provide for the other. This linkage provides a set of probabilities that will allow us to evaluate our investment future as the tectonic plates of technology, globalization, demographics, and debt evolve.

Now let's look at financial markets and a U.S.-only 60/40 portfolio (a reference anchor in *Bogle on Mutual Funds*) and see the range of potential returns as the tug-of-war between transformative AI and the rising burden of fiscal deficits unfolds.

FINANCIAL MARKETS IN THE *AI TRANSFORMS* SCENARIO: SMOOTHER SAILING

Both stocks and bonds perform well in this more optimistic scenario. Figure 9.4 presents the median (or 50th percentile) return from the thousands of simulated paths in this potential future. (I will come back to deviations from these numbers when we provide actual portfolios, as the dispersion across the returns can matter as much as the "average.")

Bond market: *Solid returns.*

Looking back from the year 2035, there have been Fed tightening and easing cycles just like in the past. For the period, though, the rise in real interest rates, not inflation, is the key driver of these higher nominal rates for bond portfolios. Positive real interest rates endure (e.g., so-called r* or the neutral rate[5]) because trend growth is higher, not because of higher inflationary pressures. Bonds have positive inflation-adjusted yields not because of bond vigilantes, but rather because of higher growth as was the case in the 1990s.

Equity market: *Solid returns.*

Despite episodic market corrections and spikes in volatility, stock fundamentals on average live up to their lofty 2025 expectations in the *AI Transforms* Scenario. In fact, with real GDP averaging near 3% in this

Figure 9.4   Investment returns will differ depending on the tug-of-war's victor.

(a) Average yield on U.S. 10-year Treasury bond. (b) U.S. stock market, average annualized total return.

Source: Author's calculations and simulations. The bars for the future turns represent the median (or 50th percentile) return from thousands of individual future scenarios

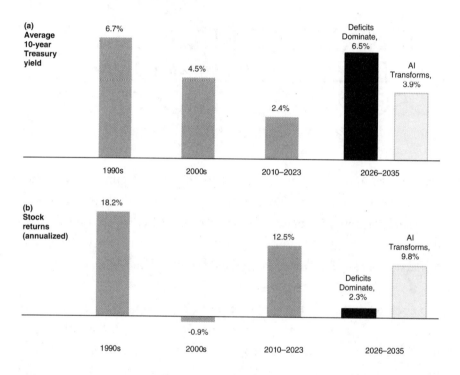

scenario, stock returns center around 9–10% per year, near their historical averages. While valuations are elevated at this time in 2025, it is the *investment returns* (dividend yield and earnings growth) that matter most for the next decade. Historically, a productivity surge has tended to boost earnings growth and corporate America's capacity to pay dividends.

In this scenario, changes in stock-market valuation are the wildcard. For example, in the 1990s, the U.S. stock market returned, on average, 18.2% per year as the dot-com revolution raised productivity and earnings growth. But only 10.8 percentage points of that figure came from earnings growth and dividends.[6] The rest came from a surge in valuations that created a stock market bubble. In the early 2000s, the bubble collapsed. This change in investor sentiment depressed stock market returns through the first decade of the twenty-first century.

My framework suggests that valuations would see less "reversion to the mean" should AI transform the economy. Stocks still underperform for a time in the late 2020s, but history shows that valuations (such as price–earnings ratios) can rise from there during a period of technological change. That does not rule out market corrections along the way, but my framework reveals that there need not be a reversion to some long-run average if economic fundamentals are changing. With strong economic growth, there will be less inflationary pressure from rising fiscal deficits in the "AI Transforms" scenario. This, too, would support higher stock market valuations.[7]

SURPRISE WINNERS WHEN AI TRANSFORMS: VALUE STOCKS

Interestingly, value stocks—not technology companies—might outperform in this future scenario. This is for two reasons. First, research shows that during past technological revolutions, early gains often concentrated in established technology leaders before diffusing more broadly.[8] For instance, during the 1990s, healthcare providers and financial institutions benefited significantly from advancements in computing and telecommunications. The electrification of the U.S. economy in the 1920s spurred rapid growth in industries such as manufacturing and transportation, demonstrating that the diffusion of general-purpose technologies (GPTs) benefit sectors beyond their immediate origin (which, of course, is a defining criterion of GPTs).[9]

Recalling the *J-curve*, the difference in returns between growth stocks and value stocks tends to mirror an "inverse" J-curve due to these developments. If AI proves transformational, its benefits will accrue to the consumers of AI, including value-based companies whose relative valuations are lower than technology companies.

Second, the massive investment during a GPT's diffusion through the economy means that new entrants into the technology field can increase competition for the early leaders in the technology field. This so-called creative destruction can reduce the returns on equity for the average "growth" company. For instance, during the rise of the early automobile industry between 1900 and 1908, nearly 500 automobile manufacturers entered the industry—and more than 250 exited.[10] By comparison, there were 1,812 newly funded AI companies globally in 2023, taking the total number of AI companies since 2020 to more than 5,000.[11]

FINANCIAL MARKETS IN THE "AI DISAPPOINTS, DEFICITS DOMINATE" SCENARIO: ROUGHER SEAS

Echoing the position of the French fleet at the Battle of the Nile, the stock and bond markets are generally unprepared for this scenario. Bond yields are higher after a period of upward adjustment, which provides higher income for balanced portfolios. Contrary to conventional wisdom, diversified bond portfolios reward investors in an era where "Deficits Dominate" scenario (someone has to fund the growing U.S. government debt) but bond volatility is higher.

The U.S. stock market, on the other hand, experiences materially lower returns, with nearly a "lost decade" in returns through the first half of the 2030s given weaker U.S. fundamentals. Earnings growth slows as GDP growth continues to sag. The benefits of diversification between stocks and bonds are a bit weaker given the inflationary shocks stemming from fiscal deficits, although that tends to be temporary until the Federal Reserve responds with higher rates to quell any rise in inflation expectations.

Bond market: *Higher yields and income.*

After years lurking beneath the surface, ever-rising structural deficits begin to push up the bond market's expectations of future U.S. inflation by 2030. This is because the U.S. bond market begins to worry more that fiscal policymakers will never reduce spending and/or raise taxes to slow the rate of increase in annual fiscal deficits. The so-called bond vigilantes finally appear in the early 2030s, demanding higher yields on their Treasury securities. Because the fiscal deficits are structural and chronic, it turns out that they did matter after all.

But the extremely high inflation of the 1970s does not repeat in this "Deficits Drag" scenario. Having learned from its lesson from that traumatic episode, the U.S. Federal Reserve attempts to neutralize fiscal-led inflationary pressures with higher short-term rates. The Federal Reserve maintains its hard-earned credibility, rising to the fiscal challenge in maintaining "sound money." But that has made growth a bit slower as a result.

Equity market: *Lower returns and risk of lost decade.*

For the stock market, corporate earnings growth and its capacity to pay dividends—two of the three building blocks of stock market returns—deteriorate. Stock prices have had to contend with higher discount rates on weaker cash flows. The third building block, valuation changes, is more of a wildcard. That said, my framework suggests that valuations and stock market sentiment are likely to fall over time as they are tied to technological progress, a negative for stock market returns in the "Deficits Drag" scenario.

It was well known in 2025, for instance, that to justify those U.S. stock-market valuations, corporate earnings would need to grow by about 40% per year through 2027, a pace that would have been unprecedented in economic history.[12] AI has not helped meet those incredibly rosy expectations, another case consistent with what Professor Robert Shiller refers to as *Irrational Exuberance*, the title of his popular 2000 book. Stock returns have, on average, been only slightly ahead the rate of inflation, a disappointment for those investing for retirement and other life goals.

TUG-OF-WAR RETURNS FOR THE 60/40 PORTFOLIO

As you probably suspected, the average returns for the U.S.-only 60/40 portfolio differ significantly in these two scenarios. It should be said that both are expected to achieve positive returns that exceed the rate of inflation over the future 10-year period. For the "AI Transforms" scenario, the returns are solid at 7–8% (7.6% in Figure 9.5), near the historical averages we discussed earlier. For the "Deficits Drag" scenario, the returns are weaker given lower U.S. earnings and stock market returns.

Overall, this range of annualized returns is well within the range experienced in the past. That is good news. But the "Deficits Drag" scenario is somewhat concerning from a risk perspective. As Figure 9.5 illustrates, there's greater than a 1-in-3 chance that the nominal returns will fail to outpace inflation over the next decade should AI disappoint.

Figure 9.5   U.S.-only 60/40 portfolio returns under each mega-trend scenario.

Source: Author's calculations and simulations. Annualized returns represent the median from a distribution of thousands of simulations

June 2027–June 2037		Traditional U.S.-only 60/40 stock/bond portfolio		Megatrends-aware portfolio	
		Annualized Return	Odds of negative real return	Annualized Return	Prob. real return is negative
Future return environment	AI Disappoints, Deficits Drag	3.6%	38%	5.0%	19.4%
	AI Transforms, Productivity Surges	7.6%	5%	7.1%	2.6%

TWO CHOICES IN "STAYING THE COURSE"

As investors, I believe there are two viable options in response to this bifurcated financial outlook. Each option shares the investment principles that we discussed in the previous chapter.

Stay the Course: Option A

The first option is to make no adjustments whatsoever to one's asset allocation. Thinking of the Battle of the Nile, it would be akin to a captain choosing to steer clear of the bay and to avoid entirely the battle. This approach can be an appropriate choice for investors who meet one of the following conditions:

- An investor unwilling to experience any returns that deviate from their long-run asset allocation (e.g., someone who does not want to have any "active" performance risk).

- An investor who believes that the U.S. stock markets' current assessment that AI is highly likely to become transformational is accurate (e.g. the S&P500 Index, by my calculations, is assigning an approximately 80–90% probability based on year-end 2024 prices). In other words, one may believe strongly that efficient markets and the wisdom of crowds will prevail.

These are valid preferences. The course of action would be equivalent to abstaining from the Battle of the Nile, like a conscientious objector. If you share these preferences and beliefs, you will receive no judgment from me. This is your portfolio. The set-it-and-forget-it 60/40, like all other investment strategies, will be exposed to future volatility anywhere on the high seas of investing.

Stay the Course: Option B

There is likely a group of investors who may not share such preferences. If you are wondering, I am one of those investors. For investors willing to take some risk to reduce the exposure to the "AI Disappoints, Deficits Drag" scenario, there is another option consistent with "stay the course."

Following probability-based decision-making, this approach considers two investment choices that can be implemented with low-cost index ETFs or mutual funds. These choices are ones I explored in the previous chapter when I discussed potential "dogma" regarding a long-term investment program. The two actionable—and moderate—portfolio allocation considerations for an investor that seeks a balance between capital appreciation and stability are the following:

- **Increase one's strategic allocation to value stock funds** and non-U.S. equity funds within one's stock allocation (recall Myth #2 from the last chapter). Value stocks have historically outperformed during a period of rising interest rates and economic uncertainty. International

166

diversification can reduce the reliance on U.S. growth and the exceptional outperformance of the U.S. stock market over the past two decades, especially if AI disappoints. If AI transforms, many countries will benefit, especially other developed markets with elevated debt levels. The same is likely for emerging markets that have deeper AI-related capabilities, most notable China and India.

- **Increase one's strategic allocation modestly to bonds** based on probability-based conservative asset allocation (recall Myth #3 in Chapter 7). With bond yields expected to rise in the "Deficits Drag" scenario, increasing fixed-income exposure offers a compelling way, overtime, to learn positive, net-of-inflation returns. Investment-grade corporate (and municipal) bonds offer compelling risk and return trade-offs under either scenario.

How one implements these considerations in a sensible, risk-controlled way entails weighting the tug-of-war scenarios by their probabilities to better hedge different economic and market outcomes for your portfolio.[13] Like Lord Nelson in the Battle of the Nile, these conscious choices take modest risk with the goal of narrowing the range of future outcomes. The goal is not one of strict return outperformance, but one of risk management.

The end result is a well-diversified, balanced portfolio that differs somewhat from the 60/40 portfolio. I will refer to this scenario-weighted portfolios as the Megatrends-Aware Portfolio. This portfolio can be implemented in low-cost, diversified index ETFs or mutual funds. Table 9.1 summarizes the allocations of the Megatrends-Aware Portfolios. As I have done throughout for the tug-of-war scenarios, I list *ranges* for subasset allocations that include the specific quantitative (or *optimized*) allocation. For the equity allocation, a very low-cost U.S. total stock market index remains a core of the portfolio.

Table 9.1   Allocations for the 60/40 Benchmark and
the Megatrends-Aware Portfolio

Investment Type		U.S. Only 60/40	Megatrends Aware Portfolio
		Passive	Passive
Equity			
	US Broad Stock Market	60%	25–30%
	US Value	0%	15–20%
	US Growth	0%	0%
	Global ex-U.S. ("International")	0%	10–20%
	Total Equity	**60%**	**50–60%**
Fixed income			
	US Government Bonds	0%	15–20%
	US Corporate Bonds	0%	20–30%
	US Broad Taxable Bond Market	40%	0–10%
	Total Bond	**40%**	**40–50%**
Total Passive (Index ETFs)		*100%*	*100%*
Total Active Funds/ETFs		*0%*	*0%*

SOURCE: Author's calculations

ALIGNING PORTFOLIOS FOR TWO PATHS, NOT ONE

Table 9.2 shows the expected results for the Megatrends-Aware Portfolio. The median expected returns between the two portfolios are similar (6.0% versus 6.3%) across all scenarios. But the narrower dispersion in the returns for the Megatrends-Aware Portfolio is improved because it gives more appropriate weight to the two megatrend scenarios, thereby better hedging future macroeconomic risk.

Table 9.2 Megatrends-Aware Portfolio Should Reduce Downside Risk Should AI Disappoint

		Traditional 60/40 Portfolio			Megatrends-Aware Portfolio	
	June 2027–June 2037	Ann. Return	Prob. real return is negative		Ann. Return	Prob. real return is negative
Future return environment	**Deficits Drag Scenario**					
	P(upside) = 10%	3.60%	38.20%		5.00%	**19.40%**
	P(upside) = 20%	4.40%	31.50%		5.40%	16.20%
	P(upside) = 40%	5.20%	24.60%		5.80%	12.40%
	Megatrends, Probability-Weighted Scenarios	**6.00%**	**17.70%**		**6.30%**	**9.00%**
	P(upside) = 80%	6.90%	11.40%		6.70%	5.90%
	AI Transforms Scenario					
	P(upside) = 100%	7.60%	4.60%		7.10%	2.60%

SOURCE: Author's calculations from author's simulations, with the portfolio statistics reflecting the period 2027 through 2037

With a greater allocation to bonds and a diversified set of value companies, the megatrend-aware portfolio effectively shifts a meaningful share of the portfolio return to income generation (e.g., coupons and dividends) rather than price appreciation. With these allocation changes, the megatrend-aware portfolio improves downside protection in the "Deficits Drag" scenario, at the expense of also reduced upside potential should AI prove transformational.

NOT A FREE LUNCH

This portfolio is not a free lunch. Rather, it is about taking modest risk, in the form of modest allocation changes, in pursuit of narrowing the range of future outcomes over the coming decade. If this sounds like the strategy Lord Nelson deployed at the Battle of the Nile, it is. By splitting our asset allocation to account for two paths (and not one), the sum of those parts provides a portfolio that is better aligned to the coming tug-of-war scenarios.

For example, in periods of significant market volatility, the expected maximum drawdown in the "Deficits Drag" scenario is a −15.4% return in the U.S.-only 60/40 portfolio versus a more modest −9.8% in the Megatrends-Aware Portfolio.

CONCLUSION: BUILDING RESILIENCE

The balanced 60/40 portfolio has endured for more than a century, weathering wars, recessions, and bubbles. Its resilience lies in its elegant simplicity— a diversified mix of stock and bonds that captures capital appreciation and income while mitigating risk.

As we navigate the decades ahead, the tug-of-war between AI and fiscal deficits will present new challenges and opportunities. But the principles that have guided balanced investing—diversification, discipline, value—will endure. By learning from history and embracing modest adjustments, investors will be positioned for success no matter what path the economy takes.

There is another chapter to this portfolio story for those willing to take more risk. It involves active management of a different type to supplement the risk-mitigating Megatrends-Aware Portfolio. But it may not suit your personal risk tolerance. A favorite childhood movie of mine will help to see if it right for you.

NOTES

1. Foreman, L. and Phillips, E. B. (1999). *Napoleon's Lost Fleet: Bonaparte, Nelson, and the Battle of the Nile.* Roundtable Press, P.123

2. Lane, A. 2005. *The Pursuit of Victory: The life and Achievement of Horatio Nelson by Roger Knight.* An imprint of Penguin Books. P. 291. The pursuit of victory.

3. *Napoleon's Lost Fleet,* p. 131.

4. *The Pursuit Of Victory,* p. 302.

5. For more on this concept, please see Davis, J. H., Zalla, R., Rocha, J., and Hirt, J.. *R-Star Is Higher. Here's Why.* Social Science Research Network, June 14, 2023. ssrn.com/abstract=4478413.

6. Bogle, J. C. (2010). *Common Sense on Mutual Funds.* Hoboken, N.J., Wiley.

7. Historically, exceptionally strong stock market runups have not always translated into an immediate "crash," which some define as evidence of a bubble. In fact, William Goetzman (2016 NBER paper) examined various stock market episodes in the U.S. and elsewhere and found that stock markets with returns exceeding 100% or more in one year are twice as likely to double again (!) as they are to decline by 50%. This is another reason not to attempt market timing.

8. For an exceptional academic study on this topic, please see Pastor, L. and Veronesi, P. (2008). "Technological Revolutions and Stock Prices," *American Economic Review* 99, 1451–1483.

9. Conversely, our megatrends framework suggests that as much as one-half of the extraordinary outperformance of growth stocks over value stocks over the past 20 years can be explained by a lack of general-purpose technology boosting broad productivity trends. In order words, a lack of GPT has had a role in driving up the premium (i.e., price) of existing U.S. technology companies. This is an interesting and important finding that requires more research that I will not pursue here. If AI proves to be a broad-based GPT, that would also support value stocks given what I note here.

10. Nairn, A. (2018). *Engines That Move Markets.* Harriman House, 2nd edition, page 213.

11. Data comes from Chapter 4 of Stanford University's *Artificial Intelligence Index Report 2024.*

12. "Economic payoff of AI is coming—but it's not here yet," Vanguard.

13. These active choices are limited to the conditions from the table we discussed in Chapter 7 and, at the margin, are more restrictive than the guidance discussed in *Bogle on Mutual Funds*. Specifically, I optimize the probability-weighted returns from the tug-of-war scenarios to best balance the trade-offs between portfolio return and risk for an investor with a moderate tolerance for "active" risk in deviating from his or her long-term strategic asset allocation. That allocation I have defined here as a U.S.-only, all-indexed, market-capitalization 60/40 portfolio since that was a reference point provided in *Bogle on Mutual Funds*.

CHAPTER TEN

A VICTOR'S PORTFOLIO, ACT II: CHOOSE WISELY

INDIANA JONES

The highest-grossing film in 1989 was director Steven Spielberg's blockbuster *Indiana Jones and the Last Crusade*. As a teenage fan of the Indiana Jones franchise, I remember waiting in long lines at the movie theater to watch Indiana (Indy) Jones, played by Harrison Ford, and his father, played by Sean Connery, travel to modern-day Turkey to search for the Holy Grail. As with any good action movie, they were not alone in their search. Other menacing characters sought the Holy Grail, a chalice from the Last Supper believed to hold special healing powers.

Toward the movie's climactic end, Indiana Jones and his father find the temple that holds the chalice. They meet an Arthurian knight (in Hollywood style, still alive since the Crusades), stationed in front of an altar filled with chalices. Most chalices are made of gold and adorned with sparkling jewels and other ornate embellishments. Then an adversary, hoping to secure the chalice for the forces of evil, barges into the room. "Which one is it?" he demands. The knight responds, "You must choose. But choose wisely. For as the true grail will bring you life, the false grail will take it from you."

The adversary selects a bejeweled, ornately engraved chalice. "This certainly is the cup of the king of kings," he says. He fills the cup and drinks from it. He chokes, collapses. He disintegrates into a pile of dust. "He chose … *poorly*," the knight states simply. Indy approaches the altar with some trepidation and then selects a simple chalice in the hopes of healing his dying father. "That's the cup of a carpenter," he says. He drinks from it. "You have chosen wisely," the knight says.

MANAGING MEGATREND RISK AND ACTIVE MANAGEMENT

Rarely have I found investment lessons in movies. They are for entertainment and enjoyment. I certainly didn't see any investment lessons when I watched *Indiana Jones* as a teenager. But when someone asks me about the role of active management in a portfolio, I reminisce about that movie scene. Although the stakes are (mercifully) lower, the knight's injunction to choose wisely contains some lessons as to both the allure—and the challenge—of active management.

The previous chapter's portfolio strategy, inspired from the Battle of the Nile, was about managing risks. It was Act I in a two-act play.

The Megatrends-Aware Portfolio from Act I favors segments of the U.S. stock and bond markets such as value stocks and corporate bonds (or, for tax-sensitive investors, municipal bonds) designed to best balance future investment risk from the coming tug-of-war between AI and rising fiscal deficits.

This chapter's portfolio strategy considers the potential role that active funds and ETFs could play in our Megatrends-Aware Portfolio. I have titled this chapter Act II because, unlike in Act I, this strategy involves taking some "active" risk in pursuit of a reward. We know that the average actively managed stock fund struggles to beat an equivalent index fund after costs, largely due to high fees and efficient markets.

But there's a deeper, less obvious reason that contributes to this underperformance. This is where the Holy Grail story from *Indiana Jones* comes in. It has to do with the skewed nature of stock market returns. This dynamic in Act II leads us to maintaining low-cost index funds as a core of the Megatrends-Aware Portfolio. But it also offers investors some perspective if one is to consider active management, which we'll do here. No matter how sound our judgment, I'll share why our decision to consider actively managed funds and ETFs still requires a bit of a leap of faith, like it did for Indy.

THE NEEDLE IN THE HAYSTACK

In 2018, Professor Hendrick Bessembinder of Arizona State University published a fascinating study, "Do Stocks Outperform Treasury Bills?"[1] His findings were eye-opening: only 4% of all publicly traded U.S. stocks since 1926 have accounted for virtually *all* the stock market's long-term returns above Treasury bills. Although there have been 29,078 individual U.S. companies publicly traded between December 1925, and December 2023, fewer than 100 companies have accounted for one-third of the U.S. stock market's wealth.

Many companies on the U.S. all-time winners list have been around for nearly a century or more. They come from different industries, from Coca-Cola and Vulcan Materials (building materials) to General Electric and ExxonMobil.[2] Also on the list are somewhat newer companies like Amazon (IPO in May 1997) and Netflix (IPO in May 2002), to name but two. You can think of this so-called skewed distribution a bit like needles in a haystack, where a handful of companies account for nearly 100% of U.S. stock market returns. Conversely, more than 50% of all stocks fail to deliver positive life-time returns over a cash investment, even with dividends reinvested. As in lotteries, a few needles in the stock market account for nearly all of the return.[3]

While all this may be fascinating, I share these statistics not for stock market trivia. Rather, it is to underscore the challenge active management faces beyond its costs. Choose wisely, or face underperformance as in *Indiana Jones*. Active equity funds often hold concentrated portfolios, increasing the odds of choosing poorly. So few needles also underscore the importance of diversification. Index funds, which own "the entire hay-stack" as Jack Bogle put it, capture those elusive needles—those 4% of stocks driving market returns. In *Indiana Jones*, owning the entire haystack is equivalent to owning all the chalices in the knight's room.

Needles in Various Markets

The needles-in-the-haystack effect isn't unique to U.S. stocks. Professor Bessembinder's research shows that just 2.4% of the 64,000 global public companies trading since 1990 have generated nearly all the wealth created in global stock markets since 1990—an astonishing $75.7 trillion. Over the past 30 years, non-U.S. companies joining the likes of Apple, Microsoft, Tesla, and Wal-Mart include companies from Asia (e.g., Samsung and Taiwan Semiconductor), Europe (e.g., Nestle), and elsewhere.[4]

This needle-in-the-haystack effect reinforces the case for broad-based index investing globally. Consider the recent role of NVIDIA, the best-performing stock over the past 20 years. Without its inclusion in the S&P500 Index, the exceptional U.S. stock market performance between 2022 and 2024 would have trailed that of Europe, a decades-long laggard. One or two stocks can make that much difference. Regardless of the paths the megatrends take, the future 4% of needles may not all reside in the United States, another reason for some global diversification.

Private markets, including private equity, also exhibit this skewed pattern. A few investments (e.g., the next unicorn, the next Uber) deliver outsized returns, like a lottery ticket can. Many others fail to break even or disappear. The odds of picking individual winners—whether in public or private markets—are daunting. Some parts of the bond market, conversely, can exhibit less needles-in-haystack effects, which can mean that the odds of "choosing wisely" are less stacked against the active bond portfolio manager. That said, the zero-sum game holds for investment-grade corporate bonds, municipal bonds, and government bonds as it does for stocks. This means low costs and manager skill are as important in bonds as they are in stocks.

TWO MEGATRENDS-AWARE PORTFOLIOS: ONE WITH ACTIVE, ONE WITHOUT

In the previous chapter's Act I, we introduced a Megatrends-Aware Portfolio designed to navigate scenarios like "AI Transforms" and "AI Disappoints." That portfolio can be implemented with index funds alone, or with a mix of active and passive strategies.

Adding active strategies introduces risk but can also enhance returns—if one chooses wisely. Skilled managers can find needles in haystacks and capitalize on megatrend-driven shifts, such as changes in technology, demographics, or globalization. But the emphasis here is on *skilled* managers. The average active manager has no place in a portfolio.

INDEX FUNDS REMAIN AT THE CORE

Table 10.1 illustrates what the Megatrends-Aware Portfolio could look like with some allocation to lower-cost, skilled active managers. Given the odds that even skilled managers run the risk of missing the next 4%, the active-passive Megatrends-Aware Portfolio invests its core in index funds and ETFs even assuming we have better-than-average odds of choosing wisely. In fact, the share in indexing remains a high 55–65% to account for the long odds of even skilled managers in identifying the next 4% of companies given their outsized impact on your overall portfolio's returns.

CASE STUDY: ACTIVE EQUITY MANAGERS

In equity markets, successful active managers often adopt concentrated portfolios, focusing on their highest-conviction picks. This approach can deliver outsized returns if they correctly identify the next 4% of wealth-generating companies. Historical examples illustrate the diversity of these winners. Some companies were at the heart of past technological transformations, including General Electric (electricity and electronics), IBM (electronics and computer), and Amazon (Internet and rise of online

Table 10.1   Megatrends-Aware Portfolio, With and Without Active Funds

Investment Type		U.S. Only 60/40	Megatrends-Aware Portfolio	Megatrends-Aware Portfolio (with Top-Quartile, Low-Cost Active Funds)	
		Passive	Passive	% in index	% in active
Equity					
	US Broad Stock Market	60%	25–30%	20–25 %	
	US Value	0%	15–20%	10–15%	15–20%
	US Growth	0%	0%	0%	
	Global ex-US ("International")	0%	10–20%	5–15%	
	Total Equity	**60%**	**50–60%**	**50–60 %**	
Fixed income					
	US Government Bonds	0%	15–20%	5–10%	
	US Corporate Bonds	0%	20–30%	10–15%	20–25%
	US Broad Taxable Bond Market	40%	0–10%	0%	
	Total Bond	**40%**	**40–50%**	**40–50 %**	
Total Passive (Index ETFs)		*100%*	*100%*	*55–65 %*	
Total Active Funds/ETFs		*0%*	*0%*		35–45%

Source: Author's calculations

shopping). Yet other top-performing companies, like ExxonMobil or Proctor & Gamble, had no direct ties to those technological transformations. This underscores the importance of a manager's ability to spot opportunities across sectors. Such opportunities could arise in any market, which is why I do not specify that the 15–20% active equity allocation be confined to any specific active value, growth, or international stock fund.

If you are to consider this active-passive portfolio, you may want to consider whether the active manager would thrive more in the "AI Transforms" versus the "AI Disappoints" scenario. For example, should the "AI Transforms" scenario prevail, active growth managers that tend to specialize in earlier-stage growth companies and underweight technology incumbents (in the hopes of finding the next Amazon or NVIDIA) may be appropriate. For value managers, perhaps one would focus less on "deep value" managers who tend to focus on more cyclical securities and instead favor those that may excel in separating AI "winners" outside of technology (assuming the market has not efficiently done that). These are not quantitative solutions but rather qualitative factors to consider.[5]

CASE STUDY: ACTIVE BOND MANAGERS

Although the challenges of active management apply to bonds too, the share allocated to active bond strategies is somewhat higher here (I start with 20–25% of the total 40–50% bond allocation, although one could go higher). In a higher interest rate environment, skilled bond managers would be expected to navigate volatility and identify mispriced securities in the corporate (or municipal) bond markets, which can exceed the number of securities in the U.S. stock market. Personally, I would be focusing on managers that focus more on security selection, with any adjustments for interest rates and credit quality done to best manage macroeconomic risks as the tug-of-war unfolds.

CONCLUSIONS: ACTIVE STRATEGIES CAN PLAY A ROLE

Today, a reliable, quantitative framework does not exist to identify managers ahead of time who will outperform. How then can I—a card-carrying economist—invest some of my own portfolio in active strategies? It's a question of conviction in choosing wisely—a few active stock and bond strategies run by talented managers held for the long term at a reasonable cost. My conviction has been forged by my 20-year-plus experience in working with portfolio managers as part of their investment process, as well as the work of my colleagues in using a time-tested, rigorous process that combines science and judgment to identify skill.

The all-index Megatrends-Aware Portfolio is designed with the goal of reducing risk in the years ahead. The intention is to narrow your range of possible portfolio returns. Adding select active strategies, as I have done here, modestly increases my portfolio risk in the hopes of above-market returns. Personally, I am willing to accept periods of inevitable underperformance from these active strategies in the hope that these funds are long-term winners in the zero-sum game. And with index funds (or ETFs) as the core of my Megatrends-Aware Portfolio, I am shielded from the Arthurian knight's all-or-nothing choice in *Indiana Jones*.

NOTES

1. Bessembinder, H. (2018), "Do stocks outperform Treasury bills?", *Journal of Financial Economics*, 129(3), 440–457. https://doi.org/10.1016/j.jfineco.2018.06.004.

2. For those interested in seeing the full list of individual U.S. stocks, Professor Bessembinder publishes it on a website at https://wpcarey.asu.edu/department-finance/faculty-research/do-stocks-outperform-treasury-bills. See also https://papers.ssrn.com/sol3/papers.cfm?abstract_id=4897069.

3. For those feeling FOMO ("fear of missing out") when they hear of the latest "hot" AI or other technology stock, this is a humble reminder of the long odds in picking individual stocks.

4. For the full list, see Table 6 in https://papers.ssrn.com/sol3/papers.cfm?abstract_id=3710251.

5. Another consideration for active equity strategies would be to consider more quantitative-oriented funds that hold many more securities. Such an approach reduces the odds of "outsized" gains derived by the 4% of stocks, but like the Megatrends-Aware Portfolio itself, could reduce the odds of missing the 4% of stocks altogether.

CHAPTER ELEVEN
CONCLUSION

PRESENT DAY

More than a century has passed since that de Havilland DH-4 airplane flew over Skagway, Alaska, on that fateful day in August. Today, Skagway remains a small town with a population of only 1,240.[1] Its main industry is tourism. Every year, a long dock on the Taiya Inlet welcomes thousands of cruise-ship visitors. Many visitors tour the town's historical district and its buildings from the gold rush era that celebrate its past. Figure 11.1, taken from a cruise ship in 2013, shows the very field where the black-and-white photograph of that de Havilland DH-4 airplane was taken.

RUGGED SEAS AND RESOLVE

Skagway is the English adaptation of *sha-ka-ɢéi*, a Tlingit expression that figuratively refers to the "rugged seas in the Taiya Inlet" that result from strong northly winds.[2] Much has changed in Skagway and along the windy

Taiya Inlet since that day in August 1920. Alaska was officially granted U.S. statehood in 1959. It transitioned from a small mining town to a small tourist spot, a symbol of how economies and societies evolve as megatrends shift. Ups and downs. But in the end, the photo conveys to me a spirit of resolve.

Figure 11.1   Skagway, Alaska—yesteryear and today.
Sources: National Park Service, Klondike Gold Rush National Historical Park, Candy Waugaman's Collection, KLGO Library TA-8-8917; Getty Images

As I imagine looking out from that dock out over the Taiya Inlet, it is hard not to feel optimistic as both an investor and as an American. To be sure, the U.S. economy will, like the rest of the world, experience change in the decades to come. I am confident that the world's most resilient economy will press on as it has in the past, regardless of what the future brings.

And as investors, I have no doubt that our own resolve will be rewarded for staying the course on the market's high seas.

NOTES

1. 2020 Census Data – Cities and Census Designated Places (Web). State of Alaska, Department of Labor and Workforce Development. Retrieved October 31, 2021.
2. Thornton, T. F. (2004). *Klondike Gold Rush National Historic Park Ethnographic Overview and Assessment.* U.S. Dept. of Interior., at page 53.

APPENDIX

FRAMEWORK DETAILS FOR THE INTERESTED READER

The framework developed for this book disentangles the historical contribution of megatrends and other drivers to the *Big Four*: U.S. real GDP growth, inflation, interest rates, and stock returns. The framework is designed to assign probabilities to various scenarios. Additional details on my empirical framework can be found in a Vanguard white paper and companion academic paper:

- Vanguard white paper, *The Coming Tug-of-War,* 2024. This appendix borrows from some of the appendix in that Vanguard white paper. The published paper can be found on a Vanguard website dedicated to this Megatrends project.
- For a more academic treatment, please see Davis, Joseph H., Lukas Brandl-Cheng, and Kevin Khang, 2024. *Megatrends and the U.S. Economy, 1890–2040.* Working Paper; available at SSRN.com

Three features of the book's empirical framework are essential for understanding megatrends and their role in shaping economic and financial outcomes:

- A unique dataset that captures important historical shifts in megatrends across the U.S. and global economy.
- The explicit linking of longer-term trends (i.e., supply) with short-run cyclical variables (i.e., demand) and asset prices (i.e., stock market) in an integrated, state-of-art framework.
- An identification strategy that traces the causation (rather than correlation) of movements in each of the Big Four to their "root cause," thus providing an important economic interpretation of how megatrends have shaped the economy. The separation of trends from cycles for components of GDP and inflation aid in our sign identification of eleven unique supply, demand, and asset-price shocks. The empirical framework also accounts for time-varying volatility and covariances among all variables to account for structural shifts over time.

DATA: MORE THAN A CENTURY OF DATA ON MEGATRENDS

Most macroeconomic studies rely on data from the post-World War II period—a limitation in studying megatrends' role in the economy. The half-life of many megatrends is decades. Meaningful changes in technology, demographics, or globalization patterns might measure 10 years or more. To account for megatrends, one needs to look deep into the past. I assembled a new quarterly dataset on the U.S. economy and financial markets that begins in the first quarter of 1890. The proprietary data includes novel (hand-collected) historical data on the U.S. economy for the pre-World War II period and from other standard sources.

By extending the quarterly dataset to 1890, we gain an invaluable set of historical events that are central to developing an informed perspective on megatrends. The 1920s, for instance, witnessed high productivity growth from the diffusion of electricity as a GPT and sharp demographic changes due to restrictions on immigration. Globalization both accelerated and reversed in the period before World War II. That war produced surges in government spending and debt, trend productivity, and inflation. Even so, interest rates remained low as policymakers practiced "financial repression"—artificially suppressing rates to lower debt-burden costs. The twentieth century also saw extended periods of both deflation (such as the Great Depression) and high inflation (such as the 1970s). Over the past 130 years, the age structure of the U.S. economy has evolved because of changes in fertility, immigration, life expectancy, and the post–World War II baby boom.

TRENDS, CYCLES, AND MARKETS COMPETE IN AN INTEGRATED COMPLEX SYSTEM

We are interested in explicitly capturing time-varying trends, especially on the supply side of the economy. The supply-side trends that vary with time include technology—how the economy produces output given the production factors—and the supply of labor and capital, which are the main inputs to production. Figure A.1 lists the 15 variables featured in my empirical framework.

The 15 variables comprise five trends on the supply side (distinct from megatrends, which the next subsection defines more clearly); six business-cycle (or, "demand") variables that evolve at a faster rate; two variables that evolve closely with financial markets, and two variables—geopolitical risk and temperature change—that do not fall neatly into the above-mentioned groupings but that may have significantly affected the economy at various times. Of course, other factors can drive economic and future outcomes that we cannot account for here.

Based on these variables, the Big Four are derived as follows:

- Real GDP growth is the sum of population growth, trend growth in productivity per worker, the trend employment-to-population ratio, and the output gap.
- Inflation is the sum of the inflation gap and inflation expectations.
- The nominal federal funds rate (labeled in Figure A.1 as "monetary policy") is the sum of the real federal funds rate and inflation expectations.
- Earnings yield is the sum of the equity risk premium and the nominal federal funds rate.

Figure A.1   The 15 Variables in the Vanguard Megatrends Model™.

Notes: The table shows the definitions of the variables used in our empirical analysis, and of the Big Four: GDP growth, inflation, real interest rates, and stock market valuations.

Source: Vanguard Megatrends Model™ (Davis, Brandl-Cheng, Khang), as of May 2024

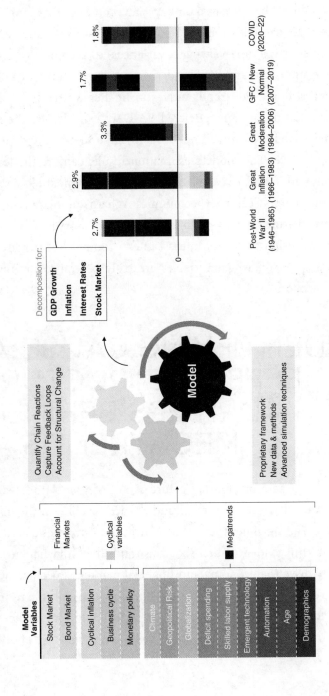

Our analysis is based on Bayesian econometric techniques that feature these 15 variables jointly. The model possesses time-varying volatility (which drives time-varying covariances) to account for structural change in relationships and the broader economy over time. By explicitly carving out the supply-side trends and featuring them with other more fast-moving variables in our sign-restricted VAR, we can identify the nature of their interrelated dynamics and develop an understanding of their relative importance. The model's estimation results capture the lead-lag correlations within and across all variables in the system and is a standard framework in empirical macroeconomics. What is unique in our setting is that we are letting the long-term trends and higher-frequency quantities—such as the business cycle of interest rates—compete. This allows us to let the data speak on which variables are truly central to driving and shaping the economy.

IDENTIFYING CAUSE-AND-EFFECT: STRUCTURAL DRIVERS BEHIND MEGATRENDS

The third and final unique feature of our integrated framework is uncovering the structural drivers behind the 15 variables in the model. This is a critical advancement versus most investment analysis conducted because it enables us to identify the "root cause and effect" of what megatrends ultimately drive the economy and financial markets. Specifically, our variables and empirical specification using Bayesian sign and zero restrictions enable us to identify three distinct types of technological change (labor-saving automation, labor-augmenting technology, and GPT diffusion) given various combinations of shocks in any quarter to labor, the capital-to-labor ratio, and productivity.

What are structural drivers, and how do they differ from any of the economic quantities observed in our model? We use fiscal deficits to illustrate these concepts. Fiscal deficits rise (and fall) over time for multiple reasons. Historically, several main drivers of fiscal deficits have included:

- recessions, which lead to an expansionary fiscal policy (such as the CARES Act of 2020 in response to COVID-19);
- wartime expenditures (such as the Lend-Lease Act of 1941 and the G.I. Bill of Rights of 1944);
- rising interest rates adding to debt servicing costs (for example, in the 1980s); and
- structural fiscal deficits tied to rising entitlement spending because of the aging population.

Let's assume we want to distinguish the first two drivers from the latter two, because the first two are transitory and tend to have an expansionary impact on the economy, whereas the latter two are tied to the economy's long-term conditions. This calls for an ability to distinguish among the four structural drivers behind rising (and falling) fiscal deficits over our sample period.

Cause-and-effect is achieved through structural VAR identification, a methodology commonly deployed in the macroeconomic literature that enables us to uncover these four main structural factors driving fiscal deficits over our sample period. Essentially, we apply a standard technique in structural VAR literature and specify a combination of restrictions to identify the structural shocks needed for quantification of their magnitudes in past, present, and future outcomes. This allows us to decompose fiscal deficits into those due to the first two drivers and those due to the latter two drivers, as illustrated in Figure A.2.

Figure A.2 Fiscal deficits are increasingly shaped by structural drivers.

Notes: The figure shows the historical contribution of structural drivers (interest rate on debt service, age-related spending) and of non-structural drivers (e.g., rising deficits during wartime or recessions) to the deviation of the fiscal deficits/GDP from their long-run average, between 1929 and 2023. Negative values in the fiscal deficit represent a fiscal surplus.

Source: Vanguard calculations, as of May 2024

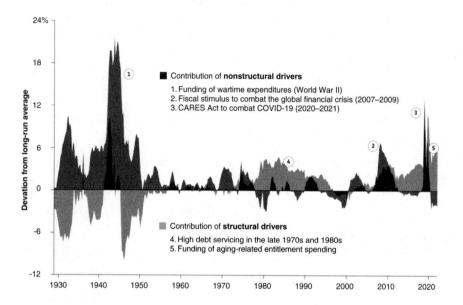

Figure A.2 shows that the latter two drivers—especially the deficits connected to finance entitlement spending—have been causing fiscal deficits to rise since the global financial crisis. The last time that structural U.S. fiscal deficits were this high was in the 1970s and 1980s, when high inflation and interest contributed majorly to debt servicing costs.

RELATIVE IMPORTANCE
OF MEGATRENDS
TO OTHER FACTORS

Megatrends can add to our understanding of the source of fluctuations observed in the short run for macroeconomic variables such as GDP growth, inflation, interest rates or the stock market. Consider the pie chart in Figure A.2. It represents the contribution of various factors to the volatility in the GDP output gap, a standard measure of "demand" and the "business cycle" in some standard macroeconomic models. The pie chart on the right represents the decomposition of GDP across the 15 factors in the Megatrends Model over the period 1891Q3 through 2023Q4.

The pie slice labeled *Megatrends* represent shocks to supply factors, including three types of technological change, demographics, structural fiscal deficits, globalization, and a few others. The pie slice labeled *Demand* includes the output gap, commodity prices, financial conditions, and two types of monetary policy (all of which are considered "demand" in the industry's standard narrative). A nearly identical picture emerges when you look at the U.S. stock market.

Figure A.3   Megatrends matter in the here and now.
Source: Author's illustration based on the Vanguard Megatrends Model™

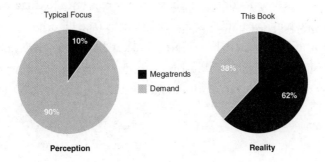

A COMPREHENSIVE APPROACH

Events in 2024 provide some perspective on the merits of explicitly accounting for megatrends in forecasting and analysis. With inflation elevated and the Federal Reserve maintaining a "restrictive" level of interest rates, a demand-only lens would have led to a straightforward forecast—namely, one of a "hard landing" as demand would need to fall (lower GDP and stock prices) to push down prices. That was the consensus forecast.

Of course, that "hard landing" didn't happen thanks to an increase in supply. Only when supply increases do outputs go up and prices go down. An increase in immigration (i.e., demographics) and an uptick in worker and firm productivity (i.e. technology) helped lower inflation, kept GDP growth strong at 3%, and boosted stock prices. The S&P 500 index set an all-time high in 2024 as a U.S. soft landing was achieved.

Recently, even Federal Reserve Chairman Jerome "Jay" Powell acknowledged the critical role that our supply-related forces have had in the soft landing, stating that "Improving supply conditions have supported this strong performance of the economy. The labor force has expanded rapidly, and productivity has grown faster over the past five years than its pace in the two decades before the pandemic … allowing rapid economic growth without overheating."[1]

Beyond a few years or more, these four forces tend to dictate most the outcomes we may care most about as investors (see Figure A.4). In a 2017 speech at the Economic Club of New York, Chairman Powell noted that "while monetary policy can contribute to growth by supporting a durable expansion in the context of price stability, it cannot reliably affect the long-run *sustainable level of the economy's growth*."[2] The italics are mine. That phrase is influenced by the four forces discussed in this book. And those forces, more than Federal Reserve policy, will likely determine where U.S. growth, inflation, and the financial markets go over the next decade.

Figure A.4   Beyond three years, only megatrends matter.

Note: The pie slice labeled Megatrends represent shocks to supply factors, including three types of technological change, demographics, structural fiscal deficits, globalization, and a few others. The pie slice labeled Demand includes the output gap, commodity prices, financial conditions, and two types of monetary policy (all of which are considered "demand" in the industry's standard narratives evolving growth).

Source: Author's illustration based on the Vanguard Megatrends Model™

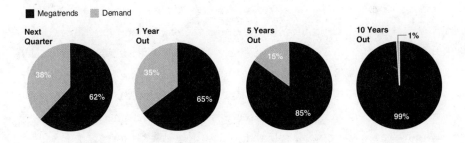

NOTES

1. U.S. Federal Reserve. 2024. "Speech by Chair Powell on the Economic Outlook." Board of Governors of the Federal Reserve System. November 14, 2024. https://www.federalreserve.gov/newsevents/speech/powell20241114a.htm.
2. U.S. Federal Reserve. 2024. "Thoughts on the Normalization of Monetary Policy," at https://www.federalreserve.gov/newsevents/speech/powell20170601a.htm.

ACKNOWLEDGMENTS

Few authors ever write a book alone. I have a long list of individuals to thank. To Bill Falloon and Wiley, thank you for your partnership in bringing this book to market and in your expert revisions and suggestions.

I want to extend special thanks to several Vanguard "crew members" who made meaningful contributions to this book. First and foremost, I want to recognize Andy Clarke, a Vanguard veteran who was a special contributor to this book. Andy is among the best writers in the financial services industry. Andy, like a skilled alchemist, you turned some of my drafts into a more compelling read—thank you. Lukas Brandl-Cheng on my Investment Strategy team in London extended the megatrends model's forecasting engine and tirelessly met with me nearly every day in developing our empirical framework early on in this project. Roger Aliaga-Diaz, the global head of portfolio construction in our Investment Strategy Group, patiently listened to my conceptual ideas and served as a critical sounding board. Thanks also to my Investment Strategy Group leadership team (the best in the business) for providing feedback on drafts, including a special recognition of Rebecca Katz for helping secure funding to aid in this book's development. Joseph Quinlan, my chief of staff, provided invaluable draft and research assistance.

Several analysts in Vanguard's Investment Strategy Group made significant contributions to specific chapters, including top-notch research. Without their tireless contributions and teamwork, this book would simply not have been possible. I want to especially recognize Adam Schickling (Chapters 2 and 6); Kevin Khang, Ollie Harvey, and Lukas Brandl-Cheng (Chapters 8 and 9); Shaan Raithatha (Chapter 5); Josefina Rodriguez (Chapters 4 and 5); Grant Fang (Chapter 3); and Xiao Xu and Andrew Patterson (Chapter 4). To everyone on this list, I was honored to be part of a special team.

A long list of current and former Vanguard crew members made valuable contributions to this book during its development. I would like to extend special recognition to Jack Brennan, Tim Buckley, Michael Carr, Paulo Costa, Rick Delfin, Joel Dickson, Nick Eisinger, Dawn Gatto, Annmarie Gioia, Fiona Greig, Doug Grim, Liz Fisk, Lara de la Iglesia, Ian Kresnak, Emmett Linn, Russ Messner, Warren Pennington, Andy Reed, James Rowley, Daniel Shaykevich, Shubhangi Shree, Andrew Shuman, Bryan Thomas, Ravi Tolani, and, finally, former Jack Bogle assistant Mike Nolan. Outside of Vanguard, I want to thank the following individuals for constructive feedback on earlier drafts of this book: Azeem Azhar, Gene Kim, Michael Riordan, and Patrick Sillup.

I want to also take this opportunity to thank several senior Vanguard leaders for their inspiration and tireless support in my 20-plus years at Vanguard. To Tim Buckley, William McNabb, Jack Brennan, Gus Sauter, Mike Miller, and Greg Davis—each of you have inspired me and countless other crew members with your servant leadership, courage, and strategic mindset. Each of you also provided tremendous support and guidance in this project. I also thank the Vanguard Board of Directors, who collectively voiced tremendous support for this project. In particular, I want to recognize André Perold for offering me sage advice and the opportunity to present some of this work at Harvard Business School. I also thank Luis Viceira of Harvard Business School for his counsel on this project.

Finally, to my family. To my parents, Joseph and Helen Davis, for loving this economist through the teenage years and every year since. Mom and Dad, your constant love and support made all the difference. To my brother Matt, for encouraging me to write this book. To my two children, Matthew and Makenna, who read early drafts and even assisted with data collection for this book during COVID-19. You each inspire me; never stop pursuing your dreams.

Most important, to my wife Elizabeth—thank you for your immaculate patience and unyielding love. You are my inspiration, my best friend, and my hero. You have been the steadfast wind in my sails every step of the way.

INDEX

Page numbers followed by *f* refer to figures. Page numbers followed by n refer to notes.

A

Acemoglu, Daron, 25, 80, 123
Active bond managers, 177, 180
Active equity managers, 178–180
The Age of Diminished Expectations
    (Krugman), 127
Aging, 3–4, 10–11, 15–16, 21, 27, 50, 62, 80–82,
    89, 108, 113, 193, xviin6. *See also*
    Demographics; Population growth
"AI buys time" scenario, 97
"AI disappoints, deficits drag" scenario, 15, 98,
    100, 119, 122, 124*f*, 125–127, 136n3,
    162–164, 166–167, 177, 180
"AI transforms, productivity surges" scenario,
    15, 119, 121, 127, 129*f*, 130, 135, 136n3,
    159, 161–162, 164, 167, 177, 180
Amazon, 4, 176, 178, 180
American Nurses Association, 28
Apple, 14, 49, 55, 57, 110, 176
ASCI White supercomputer, 49
Asia's Computer Challenge (Dedrick and
    Kraemer), 112
AT&T, 19–20, 22, 102
Augmentation, 7, 21–23, 26*f*, 27, 29, 31, 33–36,
    41*f*, 42, 81, 109, 119–120, 123, 130, 192.
    See also Automation
Automatic call distributors (ACDs), 22
Automation, 10*f*, 16, 18n9, 19, 22–28, 32–34,
    36–38, 40–42, 46, 58, 63, 76, 81,
    109, 119–120, 128, 130, 192. *see Also*
    Augmentation
Azhar, Azeem, 6
Azure AI, 62

B

Baby Boomers, 5, 30, 42, 71–72, 74–76, 81
Balanced portfolios, 156–158, 162
Balchunas, Eric, 144–145
Battle of the Nile, 151–152, 152*f*, 154, 155*f*, 162,
    165–167, 169, 174
Bayesian econometric techniques, 192
Bell, Alexander Graham, 19
Benz, Christine, 144
Bessembinder, Hendrick, 175–176, 182n2
Bogle, Jack, xi, xiv–xvi, 20, 135, 139–144, 139*f*,
    146, 154, 176
The Bogle Effect (Balchunas), 144
Bogle on Mutual Funds (Bogle), xii, 149n16,
    159, 172n13
Bond markets, 145, 159, 162–163, 175, 177, 180
Booraem, Glenn, 20–21, 23
Brandl-Cheng, Lukas, 188
Brennan, Jack, 143
Brueys, François-Paul, 152, 155–156
Brynjolfsson, Erik, 24
Buffett, Warren, 140
Bureau of Labor Statistics (BLS), 21,
    30, 32, 48n14

C

CARES Act, 193
Casey-Kirschling, Kathleen, 71–72
Certified nursing assistants (CNAs), 28–29
Chetty, Raj, 125
Clarivate Analytics Web of Science platform, 60
Clinton, Bill, 95, 100n8
Co-Intelligence (Mollick), 27

CodeFuse, 38
Computer, programmers, 36–38, 37f, 128
Computer-telephony integration (CRI) systems, 22
Comte, Auguste, 82
Cost minimization, 141–143
COVID-19, 2, 64, 65, 88, 100n7, 193
Crick, Francis, 59

D

Dalio, Ray, 4
David, Paul, 11
Davis, Joseph H., 188
De Havilland DH-4 plane, vii, ix, 11, 55, 183
Debt, x–xii, xvii, 3–7, 13, 90f, 104, 113, 148, 167, 189, 193. See also Fiscal debt; Fiscal deficits; Government debt
Debt-to-GDP ratio, 87–90, 88f
Dedrick, Jason, 112
Demographics, x–xi, 71–83, 78f, 88, 92–95, 104–105, 108–109, 113, 117, 121, 128, 134, 148, 158, 178, 189, 195–196, xixn6. See also Aging; Population growth
"Demographics is destiny" view, 3, 75–76, 80–82
Dickson, Joel, 34–35
Discipline, 142, 147, 149, 170
Disruption, 5, 36, 40–42, 120, 130
Diversification, xiv, 135, 138–139, 141, 145–147, 149n15, 156, 158, 162–163, 167, 169–170, 176–177
Dogma, 137–149, 166
Duke, Annie, xv, 156
Durst, Seymour, 99

E

Eastman, Crystal, 133
The Economic Report of the President, 13
Edison, Thomas, 12, 102
Ehrlich, Paul, 75
Electricians, 39–40, 39f
Electrifying America (Nye), 16
Emotional intelligence (EQ), 44–45
Empire of the Air, 56
Equity markets, 159, 163, 178
An Essay of the Principle of Population (Malthus), 75, 135
Exchange-traded funds (ETFs), 141–143, 145, 148n4, 166–167, 175, 178, 181
The Exponential Age (Azhar), 6

F

Federal Reserve Bank of Philadelphia, 136n4
Federal Reserve Bank of St. Louis, 45
Feedback loops, 6, 18n10, 121
Financial advisors, 17, 32–36, 48n14, 128, 143
Financial technology (fintech), 61, 63
Fiscal debt, xi, 5, 7, 15, 158. See also Debt; Fiscal deficits; Government debt
Fiscal deficits, 15, 18n9, 76, 89, 91f, 92–94, 105, 109, 115–136, 158–159, 161, 163, 170, 175, 193, 194f, 195, 197, xviin6. See also Debt; Fiscal debt; Government debt
Fiscal health, 88–94, 96
Fiscal sustainability, 92, 98
Foley, Thomas, 153
Four investment principles of Bogle, 139–147
Foxconn, 49, 50
Francis, David, 101
Friedman, Thomas L., 50
Fuller, Ida May, 85–86, 86f, 96–97
The Future of Work (white paper), 46n2

G

Gardner, Dan, xx
Gates, Bill, 110
Gaunt, John, 73
General Electric, 102, 176, 178
General-purpose technologies (GPTs), 11, 161–162, 171n9, 189, 192. See also Transformative technologies
GitHub's Copilot, 37, 62
Global AI Vibrancy Tool, 105, 107
Global Financial Crisis (GFC), 52, 64, 88, 121, 141, 194
Globalization, x–xi, 3–7, 15, 18, 45, 49–69, 53f, 68n6, 82, 105, 109, 121, 125, 128, 148, 158, 178, 189, 195, xixn6
Goliath (ship), 151, 153–154
Goodhart, Charles, 4, 50
Gordon, Robert, 3–4, 26, 116, 123
Government debt, 4, 6, 85–99, 162, xixn6. See also Debt; Fiscal debt; Fiscal deficits
Graham, Benjamin, xv, 138, 140
Grauman, Sid, 116
The Great Demographic Reversal (Goodhart and Pradhan), 4
Great Inflation, 76, 92, 94
Great Society, 93–94
Green Horizon Project, 63
Greenspan, Alan, 13, 14, 128

H
Hanel, Rudolf, 18
HMS *Vanguard* (ship), 151
Hoshi, Takeo, 111
Hughes, Thomas P., 102
Human Genome Project, 63
Hunter, Dick, 50

I
Idea multiplier, 59–61, 64–66, 103, 105, 109
Index funds, 143–145, 149n15, 175–178, 181
Industrial Revolution, 77, 79
Inflation, xi, xiii, 140, 157f, 159, 161, 163–164,
    167, 187–190, 194–197, xviin7
The Intelligent Investor (Graham), xv, 138
Interactive voice response (IVR) systems, 22–23
International Monetary Fund, 105

J
J-curve, 11–12, 14, 60, 102, 103, 109, 113, 117,
    123, 128, 134, 162
Johnson, Lyndon B., 87, 93

K
Kahneman, Daniel, 2
Karikó, Katalin, 65
Kashyap, Anil, 111
Khang, Kevin, 188
Kitces, Michael, 34
Klimek, Peter, 18
Knight, Roger, 154
Knowledge economy, 61–62
Knowledge exchange, 55, 61
Kraemer, Kenneth, 112
Krugman, Paul, 127

L
Large language models (LLMs), 38
Levinson, Marc, 54
The Life of Nelson (Southey), 152f

M
McAfee, Andrew, 24
McCarthy, John, xviin5
McCullough, David, 56
Malkiel, Burt, xv, 140, 144, xxn9
Malthus, Thomas, 75, 135
Medicare, 86–87, 94
Megathreats (Roubini), 50

Megatrends and the U.S. Economy, 1890–2040
    (Davis, et al.), 188
Megatrends-aware portfolios, 167–170, 168f,
    169f, 175, 177–178, 179f, 181, 182n5
Megatrends model, xii, 11, 18n12, 68, 100n7,
    112, 189f, 195, xviin6
Microsoft, 12–13, 23, 110, 176
Monetary policy, 68, 74, 100n7, 136n4,
    190, 195, 196
Morgan, Walter L., 137–139, 141

N
National Debt Clock, 99, 99f
*Natural and Political Observations Made upon
    the Bills of Mortality* (Gaunt), 73
Natural language processing (NLP), 29, 34
Nelson, Horatio, 151–156, 167, 169
Net-of-cost returns, 142, 167
Net-of-inflation investment return, 140, 167
Networks of Power (Hughes), 102
Neutral rate (r*), 159
New Economy, 12–13, 64, 110, 128, 158
Nursing, 28–32, 35, 36, 42, 128
NVIDIA, 177, 180
Nye, David E., 16

O
Occupational Employment Statistics
    (OES), 48n14
Occupational Information Network
    (O*Net), 45, 47n6
Occupational Safety and Health Administration
    (OSHA), 134
Orient (153), 153
Ornithological research, 56, 57f
Outside the Box (Levinson), 54

P
Palace of Electricity, 101–104
The Population Bomb (Ehrlich), 75
Population growth, x, 78f, 83n3, 96–97,
    105, 108, 135, 190. *See also* Aging;
    Demographics
Posner, Paul L., 95–96, 95f
Powell, Jerome "Jay," 196
Pradhan, Manoj, 4, 50
Principles, 43, 137–149, 165, 170
Principles for Navigating Big Debt Crises
    (Dalio), 4
Ptak, Jeff, 144

R

A Random Walk Down Wall Street
        (Malkiel), xv, 144
Rea, Clifford, 133
Reed, Andy, xviii
Reinhart, Carmen, 89
Restrepo, Pascual, 80
The Rise and Fall of Economic Growth
        (Gordon), 3–4
Rock, William, 133
Rogoff, Kenneth, 89, 96
Roosevelt, Franklin D., 86, 94
Roubini, Nouriel, 4, 50

S

Saint Louis World's Fair, 101, 103, 105, 107, 109
The Signal and the Noise (Silver), xv, 3
Silver, Nate, xiii, 3, 156
Skagway, AL, vii–xvii, 5, 7, 17, 55, 121,
        125, 183–184
Slowbalization, 50–53
Smithsonian Institution, 56
Social Security, 72, 85–87, 86f, 96–97
Solow, Robert, 11, 18n14
Southey, Robert, 152
Stagflation, 15, 50, 51, 94
Status quo view, xiii, 3–4, 15, 118–121,
        136n3, 155–156
Structural fiscal deficits, 18, 89, 91–92, 91f, 94,
        105, 193, 195. *See also* Fiscal deficits
Summers, Larry, 4, 125
Superforecasting (Tetlock and Gardner), xx

T

Technical proficiency, 44
Tetlock, Philip, xviii
Thaler, Richard H., 1–3, 5
Thinking in Bets (Duke), xiii
This Time Is Different (Reinhart and Rogoff), 89
Thurner, Stefan, 18

Time-varying asset allocation (TVAA),
        149n16
Transformative technologies, 7, 10f, 11, 15, 16,
        46, 97, 103, 134. *See also* General-
        purpose technologies (GPTs)
Trela, Rose DiMaggio, 19
Triangle of Transformation, 16–17, 130
Truman, Harry, 87

U

United States Census Bureau, 77, 83n4, 130
United States Department of Agriculture, 24

V

Value stocks, 141, 161–162, 166, 171n9, 175
Vanguard, xi, xiv, xvi, 20–21, 34, 47, 60, 135, 138,
        139, 143, 146, 188
Vanguard Megatrends Model, 18n12, 68, 189f
Vanguard's Principles for Investing Success, 148
Vulcan Materials, 176

W

Watson, James, 59
Weissman, Drew, 65
Wellington Fund, 20, 138, 139, 148n2
Westinghouse, 102
Work Accidents and the Law (Eastman), 133
The World Is Flat (Friedman), 50
World Trade Organization (WTO), 52
Wright Brothers, ix, 45, 55, 56
The Wright Brothers (McCullough), 56

Y

Yang, Kevin, 46n3

Z

Zealous (ship), 151
Zheng He, 66
Zweig, Jason, 142